What A Life!

Stories of Amazing People

Longman

Milada Broukal

What A Life!: Stories of Amazing People, Intermediate

Pearson Education, 10 Bank Street, White Plains, NY 10606

Vice president, director of publishing: Allen Ascher
Editorial director: Louisa Hellegers
Acquisitions editor: Laura Le Dréan
Senior development manager: Penny Laporte
Development editor: Andrea Bryant
Vice president, director of design and production: Rhea Banker
Associate director of electronic production: Aliza Greenblatt
Executive managing editor: Linda Moser
Production manager: Liza Pleva
Production editors: Marianne Carello/Martin Yu
Senior manufacturing manager: Patrice Fraccio
Senior manufacturing buyer: Dave Dickey
Photo research: Marianne Carello
Cover design: Elizabeth Carlson
Cover credits: Mountain climber: Solstice Photography/Artville; Violinist: Eye Wire Photography; Soccer ball/player:
    Eye Wire Photography; Writer: Eye Wire Photography; Scientist: Comstock
Text design: Elizabeth Carlson
Text composition: Publication Services, Inc.
Photo credits: p. 1, © Bettmann/CORBIS; p. 8, © Archivo Iconografico, S. A./CORBIS; p. 15, © Archivo
    Iconografico, S. A./CORBIS; p. 22, © Bettmann/CORBIS; p. 29, © CORBIS; p. 36, © Bettmann/CORBIS;
    p. 43, © CORBIS; p. 50, Courtesy of the American Council of the Ramabai Mukti Mission; p. 57,
    © Bettmann/CORBIS; p. 64, © Bettmann/CORBIS; p. 71, © FPG International LLC; p. 78, © Bettmann/CORBIS;
    p. 85, © Bettmann/CORBIS; p. 92, © Colita/CORBIS; p. 99, © AP/Wide World Photos; p. 106,
    © Bettmann/CORBIS; p. 113, © Peter Turnley/CORBIS; p. 120, © Reuters NewMedia Inc./CORBIS; p. 127,
    © Reuters NewMedia Inc./CORBIS; p. 134, Tim Hancock

Library of Congress Cataloging-in-Publication Data

Broukal, Milada.
    What a life!: stories of amazing people / by Milada Broukal.
        p.   cm.
    Contents: [3] Intermediate
    ISBN: 0-201-61998-9
    1. English language—Textbooks for foreign speakers.   2. Biography—
Problems, exercises, etc.   3. Readers—Biography.   I. Title.

PE1128.B716   2000
428.6'4—dc21   99-059443

3 4 5 6 7 8 9 10—VHG—05 04 03 02 01

CONTENTS

INTRODUCTION

What A Life! Stories of Amazing People is an intermediate reader. It is the third in a three-book series of biographies for students of English as a second or foreign language. Twenty people have been selected for this book: 10 women and 10 men. Their backgrounds and talents are very different, ranging from a fifteenth-century Italian artist to a brave African American explorer to a Guatemalan political activist. All of them have made significant contributions to the world.

Each unit focuses on one person's biography. The biographies have been arranged in chronological order; however, they can be taught in any order.

Each unit contains:

- A prereading activity
- A reading passage (1100–1200 words)
- Topic-related vocabulary work
- Comprehension exercises
- Discussion questions
- A writing activity

BEFORE YOU READ opens with a picture of the person featured in that unit. Prereading questions follow. Their purpose is to motivate students to read, encourage predictions about the content of the reading, and involve the students' own experiences when possible. Vocabulary can be presented as the need arises.

The **READING** passage should be first done individually, by skimming for the general content. The teacher may wish to explain the bolded vocabulary words at this point. The students should then do a second, closer reading. Further reading(s) can be done aloud.

The three **VOCABULARY** exercises focus on the bolded words in the reading. *Meaning*, a definition exercise, encourages students to work out the meanings from the context. The second exercise, *Use*, reinforces the vocabulary further by making students use the words in a meaningful, yet possibly different, context. This section can be done during or after the reading phase, or both. The final exercise

in this section, *Extension*, uses one of the vocabulary words to focus on a specific topic in vocabulary, such as compound adjectives.

There are several **COMPREHENSION** exercises. Each unit contains *Understanding Main Ideas, Remembering Details, Order of Events,* and *Making Inferences.* All confirm the content of the text either in general or in detail. These exercises for developing reading skills can be done individually, in pairs, in small groups, or as a class. It is preferable to do these exercises in conjunction with the text, since they are not meant to test memory.

DISCUSSION questions encourage students to bring their own ideas and imagination to the related topics in each reading. They can also provide insights into cultural similarities and differences.

WRITING provides the stimulus for students to write simple sentences about their own lives. Teachers should use their own discretion when deciding whether or not to correct the writing exercises.

What A Life! is an exciting introduction to some of history's most amazing people. Teachers may want to support their discussions with other books, magazine and newspaper articles, or videos. There are also many good websites, three of which are listed below. These sites are very informative, yet easy to navigate. They will be excellent resources for students and teachers alike.

www.encarta.com is a general, online encyclopedia.

www.biography.com is a website that specializes in biographies.

www.time.com/time/time100 features profiles of *Time* magazine's choices for the 100 Most Important People of the 20th Century. Two of the people in this book—Sigmund Freud and Bruce Lee—were among those that were chosen.

UNIT 1

LEONARDO DA VINCI
(1452–1519)

BEFORE YOU READ

Leonardo da Vinci was a genius with many extraordinary talents and abilities in many fields. What talents and abilities do you think he had? Make a list.

Intelligence _____   _____   _____

_____   _____   _____

Now read about Leonardo da Vinci.

LEONARDO DA VINCI

[1] Most people know that Leonardo da Vinci was a great painter. However, he was also a talented sculptor, musician, poet, scientist, architect, and engineer. His work had a strong influence on artists throughout Europe, and his scientific ideas were centuries **ahead of their time.**

[2] Leonardo da Vinci was born in 1452 in the town of Vinci, near Florence, Italy. His parents never married, so Leonardo lived with his father in Florence. Over the years, he had four stepmothers and eleven stepsisters and stepbrothers. One of them was 45 years younger than Leonardo! At the age of 15, Leonardo went to work with a famous artist. He studied painting, sculpture, music, mathematics, and science. By 20, he was a master painter. Leonardo was so talented that one day one of his teachers threw down his brushes and never painted again.

[3] Although da Vinci was a great painter, he never gave up his interest in other subjects. He liked to do research in many different areas. He wanted to understand everything he saw. Many people think of him as the first modern scientist because he liked to **make observations** and look for explanations for things. For example, he was one of the first people to dissect human bodies. He cut the bodies open in order to figure out how they worked. Da Vinci wrote down all his ideas and observations in notebooks. He also filled the notebooks with more than 5,000 drawings of plants, animals, and the human body.

[4] Da Vinci was a great inventor, too. His scientific research and knowledge of architecture and mathematics helped him to design many new things. For example, he drew a flying machine 400 years before the airplane was invented. He also designed an air conditioner, an alarm clock, a reading lamp, a submarine, a bridge, and many other things. In all, da Vinci designed more than 1,000 inventions. Unfortunately, he did not have time to develop many of his ideas.

[5] As a matter of fact, da Vinci started many projects that he never finished. He was always more interested in thinking about and planning projects than doing them. He was so brilliant that he quickly lost interest in one project and **couldn't wait** to start another. Because of this, he completed very few paintings. Sometimes people paid him to do a painting or a sculpture but he never did it. Other times he started the work, but he never finished it. Some people got tired of waiting, so they hired someone else to finish his work.

[6] The pieces that da Vinci completed were magnificent and unique. He created a new, more realistic style of painting. At that time, when artists painted people, they looked **flat.** When da Vinci painted people, they looked real. No other artist of his time painted people or animals as well as da Vinci. His famous painting, the *Mona Lisa,* is a good example of this style. Da Vinci took four years to paint the *Mona Lisa.* Unfortunately, the man who ordered the painting didn't like it and refused to pay him. However, ten years later, da Vinci sold it to the King of France for 492 ounces of gold (about $300,000). The King hung it in the Louvre palace in Paris. Today the *Mona Lisa* still hangs in the Louvre, which is now a museum.

[7] Often, da Vinci painted in religious buildings, like churches and monasteries. In 1495, he painted another of his greatest paintings, *The Last Supper*, on the dining

room wall of a monastery. It took him three years to complete it. People came to see it even before it was done. They admired the painting because it showed the emotions of the people in the **scene.** People also liked the bright colors that da Vinci used. Unfortunately, the painting had problems. In just a few years, the paint started to **peel** off the wall. Later, the people in the monastery made a doorway that went right through the painting. The rest of *The Last Supper* was almost destroyed when foreign soldiers threw stones at it. Fortunately, it has been repaired.

8 Da Vinci was greatly admired for his artistic talent and his skill in many areas. However, some people probably thought he was quite strange. He was a very mysterious, **private** man. He wrote backwards in his notebooks so nobody could read what he wrote. Many people thought that his scientific experiments were some kind of **evil** magic. He was also left-handed. At that time, some people believed that being left-handed was the sign of the devil.

9 Most people liked and admired da Vinci. He was a strong and handsome man. He was also generous to his friends, both rich and poor. Although he never married, he **adopted** a son and he was a very good father. People invited him to parties because he was very entertaining. He talked about interesting things and people laughed at his clever jokes. He was also a great musician. He sang well and played an instrument that he had invented. Da Vinci was always well dressed, although he liked to wear unusual clothes. He wore short robes when everyone else wore long ones and loved to wear pink.

10 Da Vinci had some other unusual habits for his time. He was extremely clean when many people were not. He even hated to have paint on his fingers. He was also a vegetarian because he did not believe in killing animals. He used to buy birds just to let them free and to study their flight.

11 During his lifetime, da Vinci traveled to all the great cities of Italy and did many different kinds of work. Once, when he was trying to get a job, he made a list of 36 different jobs he could do. In addition to working as an artist, he had also worked as an architect and engineer. He designed buildings and canals and he figured out how to change the direction of rivers. At one point, he was a military **adviser** to the Duke of Milan.

12 Later in life, Leonardo da Vinci went to Rome to work for the pope. However, he was unhappy there because the younger artists were given more work than he was. As da Vinci grew older, he stayed alone more and more. Although people admired him, many didn't understand him because his ideas were far ahead of his time. Da Vinci spent the last years of his life working for King Francis I of France. He made architectural designs, worked on engineering projects, and entertained the king with all his ideas. He also worked on his notebooks so they could be published after his death. Da Vinci died peacefully on May 2, 1519, at the age of 67.

VOCABULARY

◆ MEANING

What is the best meaning of the underlined words? Circle the letter of the correct answer.

1. Da Vinci <u>adopted</u> a son.
   a. was nice to a child
   b. took someone else's child as his own
   c. offered to become a child's private teacher

2. The people in the <u>scene</u> looked real.
   a. view of a place
   b. type of activity
   c. area where people get together

3. Da Vinci <u>made observations</u> in order to understand the world around him.
   a. built a machine for looking at the stars
   b. read many books on a subject
   c. looked carefully and noticed things

4. Da Vinci's ideas were <u>ahead of their time</u>.
   a. very important and expensive
   b. modern; not used by most people until later
   c. useful, but dangerous

5. Da Vinci worked as a military <u>adviser</u>.
   a. someone who gives opinions to others
   b. someone who fights against the government
   c. someone who designs and produces things

6. Da Vinci <u>couldn't wait</u> to start another project.
   a. did a good job with something
   b. spent a lot of time doing something
   c. was very excited to do something

7. The paint started to <u>peel</u> off the wall.
   a. lose its color
   b. wash away
   c. come off in small pieces

8. Other artists made people look <u>flat</u> in their paintings.
   a. smooth and even
   b. full and round
   c. real

9. Da Vinci was a very <u>private</u> man.
   a. enjoyed being with people
   b. didn't like to talk about himself
   c. didn't like to work

10. Some people thought da Vinci's scientific experiments were some kind of <u>evil</u> magic.
    a. interesting
    b. funny
    c. very bad

◆ USE

Work with a partner and answer these questions. Use complete sentences.

1. What are some things that are *flat*?
2. Why do some people *adopt* children?
3. Who are some *evil* characters in movies or stories?

4. What fruits or vegetables do you *peel*?

5. What are some examples of people or things that are *ahead of their time*?

6. Who would you choose as an *adviser*?

◆ EXTENSION: MAKE AND DO

Look at the sentences from the reading:

> Many people think of him as the first modern scientist because he liked to **make** observations.

> He liked to **do** research in many different areas.

Many languages have only one verb for *make* and *do*. In English, these two verbs are found in many fixed expressions. Often, we use *make* when we create or build something. We use *do* when we perform or act something. In many cases, there are no clear rules for which word to use.

Write *make* or *do* next to these words and expressions.

1. _____ a mistake   6. _____ a difference

2. _____ a choice   7. _____ homework

3. _____ business   8. _____ a favor

4. _____ money   9. _____ a discovery

5. _____ harm   10. _____ peace

Use each expression in a sentence. Then, make a list of your own expressions with *make* and *do*. Whenever you hear a new expression add it to your list.

COMPREHENSION

◆ UNDERSTANDING MAIN IDEAS

Circle the letter of the best answer.

1. Paragraph 3 is mainly about the fact that da Vinci _____.
   a. was a great painter
   b. was interested in science
   c. kept notes and drawings of his observations

2. The main topic of paragraph 6 is _____.
   a. how other artists painted
   b. da Vinci's style of painting
   c. the King of France's attitude toward da Vinci

3. The main topic of paragraph 9 is _____.
   a. da Vinci's son
   b. da Vinci's parties
   c. da Vinci's interesting qualities

4. The last paragraph is mainly about _____.
   a. why da Vinci was unhappy in Rome
   b. how da Vinci spent the last years of his life
   c. what people's attitudes were toward da Vinci

◆ REMEMBERING DETAILS

Circle *T* if the sentence is true and *F* if it is false.

	True	False
1. Da Vinci made more than 10,000 drawings of plants, animals, and the human body.	T	F
2. Da Vinci's studies in math and philosophy helped him to design many inventions.	T	F
3. Many of da Vinci's paintings were never finished.	T	F
4. The *Mona Lisa* is a good example of how da Vinci made people look real.	T	F
5. Da Vinci liked to wear long robes, even though most people wore short robes.	T	F
6. Da Vinci worked as an architect, an engineer, and an artist.	T	F

◆ ORDER OF EVENTS

Number the sentences 1–6 to show the correct order.

____ Da Vinci painted the *Mona Lisa*.

____ Da Vinci lived with his father in Florence.

____ Da Vinci studied with a famous artist and learned painting, sculpture, music, and science.

____ Da Vinci worked as an architect and engineer for King Francis I.

____ Da Vinci went to Rome to work for the pope.

____ Da Vinci painted *The Last Supper*.

◆ MAKING INFERENCES

The answers to these questions are not directly stated in the passage. Circle the letter of the best answer.

1. The passage suggests that da Vinci _____.
   a. didn't do much with his life because he never finished anything
   b. would have been a better painter if he had concentrated on art alone
   c. could accomplish great things in many areas

2. The passage implies that _____.
   a. in his work and habits, da Vinci was quite different from other people
   b. da Vinci was selfish and people didn't like him
   c. da Vinci tried to follow the style of other artists of his time

3. The passage concludes that da Vinci _____.
   a. worked very quickly on his paintings and produced many
   b. was slow to produce a completed painting because of his other interests
   c. was better at inventing than painting

DISCUSSION

Discuss the answers to these questions with your classmates.

1. Leonardo da Vinci was successful at many different things. Who are some people who are talented and successful in different fields?
2. Would you prefer to have one career or several different careers in your life? Give reasons.
3. Leonardo da Vinci adopted a son even though he wasn't married. Do you think that single people should be able to adopt children?

WRITING

On a separate piece of paper, write a paragraph or more about the career you would like to have and why.

Example: *I would like to be a teacher. I decided I wanted to be a teacher when I was in high school because I had a great history teacher.*

UNIT 2

PETER
THE GREAT
(1672–1725)

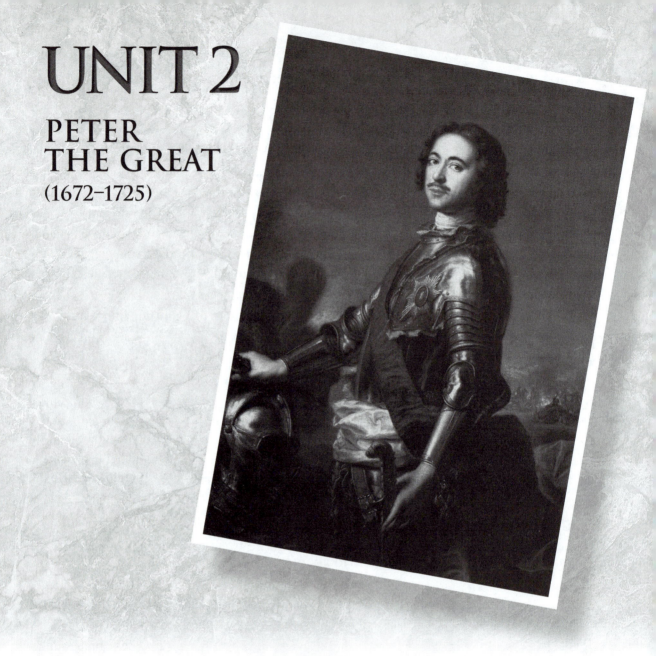

BEFORE YOU READ

Peter the Great was the first Russian leader to travel outside of his country. He traveled around Europe and brought many new ideas and changes to Russia. Discuss these questions with a partner.

1. Which leader has made great changes in his or her country in the past? What were the changes?
2. Which leader is making great changes now? What are the changes?
3. What kinds of changes would you like to see the leader of your country make?

Now read about Peter the Great.

PETER THE GREAT

[1] Peter the Great was one of the most famous tsars in Russian history. (*Tsar* is the word for a male ruler of Russia before 1917.) Although he was often cruel, no one can **deny** that he changed his country's future forever. When Peter was born in 1672, the tsar and the rich and powerful noblemen ruled Russia. They were cruel, **uncivilized,** and uneducated. At that time, Russia didn't have schools, hospitals, or factories. There were no courts of law or systems of government. Most people lived in poverty, **misery,** and fear.

[2] Peter's father, Tsar Alexis, died when Peter was four years old. There was a lot of fighting between his family and the noblemen. They didn't agree about who should be tsar. Many members of Peter's family were killed. Peter and his mother escaped and lived in a small village. Eventually Peter ruled with his half-brother Ivan and his half-sister Sophia. After Ivan's death in 1696, Peter ruled alone.

[3] Peter was unique in many ways. He was six feet eight inches tall and very handsome. He had a lot of energy and great physical strength. Peter was wild, and he sometimes had bad manners. But he was very bright and he wanted to learn about everything. Every day he added to his knowledge and improved his skills. He loved to play games of war and also liked ships and sailing. He enjoyed hard work and building things with his hands. Peter also liked ordinary things. He liked to dress in old, simple clothing. He had a huge appetite, but liked to eat simple foods such as bread, cabbage soup, and cold meat. Peter hated formal **occasions** and

behavior. He refused to allow people to kneel to him just because he was the tsar.

[4] In those days, there were great changes in European culture, science, and education. However, the noblemen in Russia did not want change. They didn't travel outside Russia and they didn't want foreigners in their country. There was a group of Europeans in Russia who worked as government and military advisers. Peter knew many of them. Several of these Europeans were his closest friends.

[5] Peter wanted Russia to be as great as the European countries. He decided to go to Europe to learn everything he could. But, he did not want to travel as the leader of a country. He wanted to be free to study and learn. So he took a large group of men with him and **disguised** himself as a common soldier. It wasn't easy to hide the huge and powerful Tsar of Russia, and soon everyone in Europe knew about the traveling Russians. Their customs and clothing were very **peculiar.** However, many people were most upset by their bad manners. For example, they completely destroyed a beautiful English country house where they stayed. They used chairs to make fires, tore up sheets and beds, shot their guns at **priceless** paintings, and ruined the beautiful gardens.

[6] Peter was as bad as his men. Nevertheless, his travels were a great success. Peter's dream was to create a powerful Russian navy, so he had to learn shipbuilding. He worked for four months in a shipyard in Holland. Then he went to England and worked in a shipyard there. Everywhere he went, he asked questions and learned more. He learned watchmaking and studied the human body. In fact, when he returned to Russia,

he even helped doctors perform surgery. Peter learned many other things in England. The Bishop of Salisbury taught him about religion and government. King William III ordered his ships to have a pretend sea battle so Peter could learn about military command. Peter sent many, many things to Russia—machinery, scientific equipment, and even an English **coffin.** He hired hundreds of specialists, such as engineers, doctors, shipbuilders, naval officers, and technicians to go back to Russia with him.

7 When he returned to Russia, Peter wanted things to change quickly. As tsar, Peter had complete power over his people and he used this power to make them change. Often he was cruel and heartless. If people didn't do what he ordered, he cut off their hands, beat them, or killed them. He even ordered his own son, Alexis, to be killed because Alexis didn't agree with his ideas.

8 Peter wanted everything to change— the government, the military, and religion. He built canals, factories, schools, hospitals, and museums. He changed the calendar and the alphabet. He developed a new system of government and started Russia's first newspaper. He even changed what people ate. Many Russians were **starving,** but they didn't eat potatoes. People called them the "devil's **root.**" But Peter helped them change their minds. Many of Peter's changes cost a lot of money. So he taxed the Russian people until they had nothing left. They paid taxes on everything from boots to drinking water.

9 He also wanted to make changes in people's personal lives. For example, at that time Russian men had beards; European men did not. So Peter passed a law that all men had to shave off their beards. If a man wanted to keep his beard,

he had to pay a tax. Peter wanted the rules to be followed, so sometimes he took a razor and removed the men's beards himself. Peter did not like the noblemen's long robes either. First he cut off the sleeves of the robes. Then he made the noblemen kneel down and he cut the robe where it touched the floor. The noblemen were very upset to see their beautiful robes cut. Soon Peter passed a law that all men and women had to dress like Europeans.

10 Peter greatly improved the lives of Russian women. At that time, men had complete power over women and often treated them badly. Women were not allowed to be out alone. They hid their bodies under a lot of clothing and painted their teeth black. In addition, fathers chose their daughters' husbands. Peter said women had to become part of the modern world. He made men and women eat meals together and go to parties together. Women were forced to wear European clothes and were no longer allowed to paint their teeth. And for the first time, women could choose their own husbands.

11 In addition to changing and rebuilding Russia, Peter wanted to get more land for his country. He went to war with Sweden, and took over a lot of land in the area. He built a new capital city, Saint Petersburg. It was a cold, wet, and empty place, but Russia needed a port city for its navy. Saint Petersburg was called "the city built on bones." Thousands of men worked for almost 10 years. Conditions were so bad that 200,000 men lost their lives. When it was completed, it was one of the most beautiful cities in the world.

12 Peter continued to build and modernize Russia right up to his death at the age of 53. Peter the Great's force and energy made his country into a modern power and made him into a legend.

VOCABULARY

◆ MEANING

Match the words with their meanings.

___ 1. uncivilized	a. box used to hold a dead body
___ 2. occasion	b. suffering or dying because there is no food
___ 3. priceless	c. strange, unusual
___ 4. starving	d. great unhappiness
___ 5. coffin	e. part of a plant that grows underground
___ 6. root	f. very valuable
___ 7. peculiar	g. having bad manners; uncultured
___ 8. misery	h. special event or ceremony
___ 9. deny	i. to change the usual appearance of someone or something
___10. disguise	j. to say something is untrue

◆ USE

Work with a partner and answer these questions. Use complete sentences.

1. On what *occasions* do people usually get dressed up?
2. How can people *disguise* themselves?
3. Where are *priceless* objects often kept?
4. What can be done to help *starving* people?
5. What is a *peculiar* habit of yours?

◆ EXTENSION: THE SUFFIX *–LESS*

Look at the sentence from the reading:

> They used chairs to make fires, tore up sheets and beds, shot their guns at **priceless** paintings, and ruined the beautiful gardens.

The suffix *-less* means "not having" or "without." When you add *-less* to some nouns, they become adjectives.

(noun)   (adjective)
price + *-less* = priceless (so valuable that you can't put a price on it)

(noun)   (adjective)
penny + *-less* = penniless (without money)

Circle the words that can be made into adjectives by adding the suffix –less. If you need help, check your dictionary.

1. harm	4. use	7. food	10. sleep
2. dog	5. friend	8. home	11. meaning
3. time	6. taste	9. color	12. education

Add three of your own words with –less. Use each word in a sentence.

COMPREHENSION

◆ UNDERSTANDING MAIN IDEAS

Circle the letter of the best answer.

1. Paragraph 1 is mainly about _____.
   a. the people who ruled Russia before Peter
   b. the way Peter changed Russia
   c. Russia before Peter came to power

2. The main topic of paragraph 6 is _____.
   a. Peter learning shipbuilding because he wanted to create a powerful Russian navy
   b. all the new people Peter met in Europe
   c. what Peter learned during his travels and how it helped Russia

3. Paragraph 9 is mostly about _____.
   a. why Peter didn't like the noblemen's beards and robes
   b. how Peter forced changes on his people
   c. when Peter decided to pass some new laws

4. Paragraph 11 is mostly about _____.
   a. why and how Peter built Saint Petersburg
   b. how Peter went to war with Sweden to capture land for a port city
   c. what makes Saint Petersburg such a beautiful city

◆ REMEMBERING DETAILS

Reread the passage and answer the questions.

1. Why did Peter decide to go to Europe?
2. Why did Peter disguise himself as a common soldier?
3. What did the Europeans say about the traveling Russians?
4. What did the Bishop of Salisbury teach Peter?
5. How did Peter change the lives of Russian women?
6. How long did it take to build Saint Petersburg?

◆ ORDER OF EVENTS

Number the sentences 1–6 to show the correct order.

___ Peter the Great's son, Alexis, was killed.

___ Tsar Alexis died.

___ Peter the Great built Saint Petersburg.

___ Peter the Great worked in a shipyard in Holland.

___ Russia went to war with Sweden.

___ Peter the Great traveled to Europe.

◆ MAKING INFERENCES

The answers to these questions are not directly stated in the passage. Circle the letter of the best answer.

1. The passage implies that _____.
   a. Peter traveled to Europe because he feared for his life in Russia
   b. Peter's foreign friends in Russia influenced his decision to travel
   c. the Russian noblemen wanted Peter to travel abroad

2. The passage suggests that Peter _____.
   a. understood why people wanted to keep their old ways
   b. caused both great good and great suffering by his changes
   c. was only interested in more power and didn't care about his country

3. The passage implies that the men who traveled with Peter _____.
   a. had no knowledge of European customs
   b. didn't like the way the English treated them
   c. tried to take over the English in their own country

DISCUSSION

Discuss the answers to these questions with your classmates.

1. Was Peter the Great successful because he was sometimes cruel and heartless? Do people have to be this way to accomplish important things? Explain.

2. What are some of the great changes that have taken place in the past 50 years and how have these changes affected people's lives?

3. What custom of dress would you like to change and why?

WRITING

On a separate piece of paper, write a paragraph or more about a change in society that you think is either good or bad. Explain your opinion.

Example: *I think the use of credit cards is a bad thing. Before people had credit cards, they were more careful about how much money they spent. But now, many people spend too much.*

UNIT 3

LUDWIG VAN BEETHOVEN

(1770–1827)

BEFORE YOU READ

Ludwig van Beethoven was one of the world's most talented and famous composers.

Discuss these questions with a partner.

1. Beethoven wrote classical music. What other classical musicians do you know?
2. Beethoven did not have a happy life. Can you imagine why this was true?
3. Do people still listen to Beethoven's music? Why or why not?

Now read about Ludwig van Beethoven.

LUDWIG VAN BEETHOVEN

[1] Ludwig van Beethoven was one of the greatest composers of all time. Much of his music was filled with great joy. Unfortunately, Beethoven's life wasn't filled with joy or happiness.

[2] Ludwig van Beethoven was born in 1770 in Bonn, Germany. He had a difficult and miserable childhood. His father, Johann, was a musician for the king. Johann started to give Ludwig piano lessons before he was four years old. Ludwig was so small that he had to stand on the piano seat to reach the piano. When Johann saw how quickly Ludwig learned, he knew his son had talent. He was determined to make Ludwig into a concert performer, and he was very demanding. He hit Ludwig's hand when he made a mistake and often woke him up in the middle of the night to make him play for friends. Ludwig continued to study, and, in 1782, he became the assistant organist for the king. He was only 12 years old!

[3] Around this time, Beethoven began composing and publishing music. He used the money that he earned to help take care of his family. His father had a lot of problems and could not support them. When Beethoven was about sixteen, he went to Vienna to study. This was every musician's dream. While he was there, he played for many important people, including the famous composer Wolfgang Amadeus Mozart. When Mozart heard him, he told his friends, "Keep your eyes on him. Someday he will give the world something to talk about."

[4] Soon after Beethoven arrived in Vienna, his mother died. He loved her very much and he was very upset by the news. In fact, he was devastated. Beethoven moved back to Bonn to help care for his younger brothers and sister. He made money by performing and giving music lessons. In 1790, Beethoven returned to Vienna. He studied for a short time with Austrian composer Joseph Haydn. Haydn was an older man and did not have the **patience** to teach the **independent,** young Beethoven. Several years later, Beethoven decided to stay and live in Vienna because all the great musicians at that time lived there. He gave many concerts and continued to compose music.

[5] Most of the well-known composers of that time worked for wealthy families. Beethoven was too independent and **rebellious** to work for anyone else, so he worked for himself. He was the first great composer to do this. His love of independence also showed in his music. Unfortunately, when Beethoven was in his late twenties, a terrible thing happened to him. He began to lose his hearing. Eventually, he would be completely deaf. Beethoven was very angry and upset by this. Sometimes he broke the strings on his piano because he hit the keys so hard to hear the notes.

[6] Music was the most important thing in Beethoven's life and his loss of hearing **tortured** him. But inside his head, the music continued to play. He continued to compose music, but it was difficult for him to perform in public. His last public performance was very emotional. When Beethoven was finished conducting, the audience began to **applaud.** But Beethoven continued to conduct because he could not hear the people applauding. Finally, one of the musicians turned him toward the audience. Now he could see how much they loved his music. He started to cry.

7 Beethoven was a brilliant composer, but a difficult man. He was **selfish** and he treated people badly. His music was so beautiful that some people cried when they heard it. He laughed at this, and thought they were stupid. Before he lost his hearing, he would walk away if people talked while he was playing. If he did not like an audience, he didn't perform at all. He could also be quite **insulting.** He wrote a song called "Praise to the Fat One," for a violinist who was overweight. Beethoven was not very attractive himself. He was short and he let his hair grow long and wild. But he knew it, and made jokes about it.

8 Beethoven was also a wild and **bad-tempered** person, especially in restaurants. Once he got so mad at a waiter that he emptied a plate of food on the waiter's head. Then he laughed loudly, as he always did. Sometimes he wrote music on the bill and then left without paying. Beethoven probably went to a lot of restaurants because he was a terrible cook. He loved macaroni and cheese, a soup made of bread and eggs, and red herring, which is a type of fish. He liked to make strong coffee and counted exactly 60 beans to the cup.

9 Beethoven usually worked early in the morning. But sometimes he stayed up all night and worked without eating or sleeping. He poured water over his head to help him stay awake, but he never cleaned it up. His room was a mess. There were dirty clothes, old pens, plates of food, and papers everywhere. His room was so dirty that all his **landlords** made him move. Beethoven himself was not very clean either. He wore the same clothes until they were so dirty that his friends had to throw them out. They usually did this while Beethoven was sleeping. They left new clothes in place of the old ones, but he never noticed. He was too busy writing music.

10 Naturally Beethoven never got married. Who would want him? He fell in love many times, however, and asked several women to marry him. Most of the women were engaged or already married. He never had children of his own, but he helped to raise his brother's son after his brother died.

11 People do not think about all these things when they hear the name Beethoven. People remember the **incredible** beauty of his music. They also remember that he helped to make classical music popular and respected around the world. Beethoven died in Vienna in 1827 when he was 57. Over 20,000 people came to his funeral. The great composer Franz Schubert helped to carry Beethoven's coffin. Schubert said that when he died, he wanted to be buried in Vienna, next to Beethoven. Sadly, Schubert died a year later, at the age of 32. He was buried next to Beethoven.

VOCABULARY

◆ MEANING

Write the correct words in the blanks.

landlord	bad-tempered	applaud	rebellious	insulting
selfish	torture	incredible	independent	patience

1. Something that is _____ is unbelievable.

2. To _____ is to hit your open hands together to show that you enjoyed a show or performance.

3. A person who owns a building and rents it to other people is a _____.

4. Being able to wait for things and deal with problems without getting angry or upset is having _____.

5. To _____ is to cause severe pain or suffering.

6. If someone is _____, he or she is angry or unhappy.

7. People are _____ when they hurt people's feelings by saying unkind things.

8. _____ people can take care of themselves without needing others.

9. People who care only about themselves and not others are _____.

10. A _____ person goes against rules and is very hard to control.

◆ USE

Work with a partner and answer these questions. Use complete sentences.

1. When *bad-tempered* people are upset, what do they do?
2. What does a *landlord* do?
3. When do people *applaud*?
4. What *incredible* thing have you seen or heard about recently?
5. What are some things that a *rebellious* person does?
6. When do you need to have *patience*?

◆ EXTENSION: COMPOUND ADJECTIVES WITH *–ED* ENDINGS

Look at the sentence from the reading:

> Beethoven was also a wild and **bad-tempered** person.

Bad-tempered is a compound adjective. Compound adjectives have two or more words with a hyphen between them. One way to form compound adjectives is to combine an adjective or number with a noun plus *-ed*.

(adjective) (noun) (compound adjective)
a man with white hair = a <u>white-haired</u> man

(number) (noun) (compound adjective)
a chair with three legs = a <u>three-legged</u> chair

Change each phrase into a phrase with a compound adjective.

Example: *A man with a bad temper*   *A bad-tempered man*

1. A person who has an open mind   _____

2. A hat which is the color of coffee   _____

3. A woman with a kind heart   _____

4. A bicycle with two wheels   _____

5. An actor with blond hair   _____

6. Clothes with a high price   _____

Add three of your own compound adjectives with –ed endings. Use each word in a sentence.

COMPREHENSION

◆ UNDERSTANDING MAIN IDEAS

Circle the letter of the best answer.

1. Paragraph 3 is mainly about how Beethoven _____.
   a. began his music career
   b. helped to care for his family
   c. met Mozart

2. The main topic of paragraph 6 is _____.
   a. how Beethoven's loss of hearing affected him emotionally
   b. why Beethoven developed his talent as a composer
   c. that Beethoven couldn't hear the audience

3. Paragraph 9 is mostly about _____.
   a. the fact that Beethoven didn't have many friends
   b. the strange way Beethoven lived
   c. Beethoven's messy room

4. The main topic of the last paragraph is that _____.
   a. people have always appreciated Beethoven's music
   b. Beethoven died in Vienna in 1827
   c. many people came to Beethoven's funeral

◆ REMEMBERING DETAILS

Circle the letter of the best answer.

1. The famous musician who first noticed Beethoven in Vienna was _____.
   a. Haydn
   b. Mozart
   c. Beethoven's father

2. Haydn taught Beethoven for just a short while because Beethoven _____.
   a. was so talented he didn't need lessons
   b. was too wild and independent
   c. had to go to work to support his family

3. Beethoven was the first great composer to _____.
   a. work for himself
   b. work for a wealthy family
   c. live outside of Vienna

4. Beethoven's loss of hearing _____.
   a. made him a better concert performer
   b. ended his career
   c. caused him to concentrate on composing music

5. Beethoven was very _____.
   a. kind to his friends
   b. bad-mannered
   c. shy and quiet

6. To stay awake while he composed at night, Beethoven _____.
   a. cleaned up his room
   b. poured water over his head
   c. invited friends to visit

◆ ORDER OF EVENTS

Number the sentences 1–6 to show the correct order.

___ Beethoven decided to live in Vienna.

___ Beethoven gave his last public performance.

___ Beethoven took piano lessons from his father.

___ Beethoven's hearing began to get worse.

___ Beethoven studied with Joseph Haydn.

___ Beethoven worked as an assistant organist for the king.

The answers to these questions are not directly stated in the passage. Circle the letter of the best answer.

1. The passage concludes that Beethoven's father _____.
   a. had no interest in his son at all
   b. loved and respected his son very much
   c. cared mostly about his son's career

2. The passage suggests that _____.
   a. Beethoven was unsuccessful because of his difficult personality
   b. Beethoven really wanted to work for a wealthy family
   c. Beethoven's independent and rebellious personality was good for his career

3. The passage implies that Beethoven _____.
   a. was so unpleasant that very few people went to his concerts
   b. was very unpleasant, but people still loved his great talent
   c. was very unpleasant, but his friends loved his kindness and generosity

DISCUSSION

Discuss the answers to these questions with your classmates.

1. Beethoven was first popular almost 200 years ago, but people today still know a lot about him and his music. Are there any performers today that will still be popular 200 years from now? Who? Why?

2. Beethoven often behaved very badly in public. Do you think famous people have a responsibility to set an example? Why or why not?

3. Many parents today push their children very hard to succeed. What do you think about this?

WRITING

On a separate piece of paper, write a paragraph or more about an independent or talented person you admire.

Example: *My friend Dalia is a very independent person. She has traveled all over the world, and now she is starting her own business.*

UNIT 4
FYODOR DOSTOYEVSKY
(1821–1881)

BEFORE YOU READ

Fyodor Dostoyevsky was one of the greatest writers in Russian history.

Discuss these questions with a partner.

1. What do you know about Russia?
2. Dostoyevsky spent some time in prison. Can you guess why?
3. What do you think Dostoyevsky wrote about?

Now read about Fyodor Dostoyevsky.

FYODOR DOSTOYEVSKY

[1] Fyodor Dostoyevsky was a very **complicated** person. Many people believe that his difficult life helped to make him a **literary** genius.

[2] Dostoyevsky was born in 1821 in Moscow. His childhood was very unhappy. His father, a doctor, was bad-tempered and violent. He believed in very strict discipline for his children. Fyodor's mother was a sweet and gentle woman. She was the only person who could control his father. When she died in 1837, Fyodor's father became even worse. He lost all control and was angry all the time. He left his job at the hospital and went to live on the family's land in the country. But he was so cruel to his workers that they eventually murdered him.

[3] Fyodor's father wanted his son to work in medicine, so Fyodor went to college in Saint Petersburg. When he was 21, he joined the army. He worked hard, and in his free time he liked to go out with his friends. Unfortunately, Fyodor spent his money foolishly and lost a lot of his money **gambling.** He earned a good salary, but he was always in debt.

[4] Dostoyevsky hated the army and left after only two years. He wanted to be a writer. He wrote a novel and sent it to some publishers. But the publishers wanted him to make some big changes. He refused. So he borrowed money and published the novel himself in 1846. The novel was called *Poor Folk*. It was a great success, and suddenly Dostoyevsky was famous. Everyone wanted to meet this talented writer. He loved all the attention, but he loved it too much. He became very **conceited.** He was often cruel to his friends and admirers. After a while, he had no friends.

[5] Dostoyevsky wanted new friends, so he joined a secret political group. The people in the group disagreed with some laws of the government. They believed in freedom of speech. They also wanted the farm workers, who were called serfs, to be free. At that time, wealthy Russians owned the serfs who worked on their land. As a boy, Dostoyevsky had spent the summer at his family's home in the country and he had become friends with the serfs. He believed very strongly that they should have rights. Dostoyevsky almost died for these beliefs.

[6] On April 23, 1849, the police arrested Dostoyevsky and other members of the political group. All of them were **sentenced** to death. They stayed in prison for eight months. On December 22, the prisoners were taken to a public place in Saint Petersburg, the capital of Russia. It was extremely cold, but the men wore only their shirts. An officer read the men's names. After each name he said "Sentenced to be shot." There was a line of coffins nearby. Someone tied up the first three men and put bags over their heads. The soldiers pointed their guns. Dostoyevsky watched in horror. There was no hope for him now. Suddenly an officer rode into the square waving a white flag. He announced that Tsar Nicolas I, the leader of Russia, had changed his mind. The prisoners were now sentenced to four years of hard **labor** in a prison camp in Siberia. Dostoyevsky was very **relieved,** but this experience tortured him. He wrote about many of these feelings in later books.

[7] For the next four years, Dostoyevsky worked as a prisoner in Siberia. The conditions were very difficult. Siberia was one of the coldest places in the world. Many prisoners suffered terribly, and many

died. After Dostoyevsky left the prison camp he had to stay in Siberia for several more years. In 1857 he married a widow with a nine-year-old son. He also joined the army and began to write *The House of the Dead,* a novel about his horrible experiences in the prison camp.

⑧ Two years later, Dostoyevsky was allowed to return to Saint Petersburg. He finished writing his book and it was eventually published. A few years later, his wife became ill and returned to Siberia. Dostoyevsky needed to raise money for his family, so he started to gamble again. Unfortunately, he only got more into debt. In 1864, Dostoyevsky's wife, his brother, and a close friend died. He was terribly depressed, and now had more financial problems. He took responsibility for caring for his brother's family and paying his brother's large debts.

⑨ Dostoyevsky moved to western Europe during the 1860s. A publisher there offered him a lot of money to write another novel. But he had to do it quickly to get the money. So he hired an assistant, Anna Snitkina, to help him. About six months later, he married her. Anna was 25 years younger than Dostoyevsky. Over the years, they had four children and a good life together. Anna took care of all of Dostoyevsky's business. She worked with the publishers and with the people he owed money. She helped him to have a happier and easier life.

⑩ During the last 20 years of his life, Dostoyevsky wrote his four most important novels: *Crime and Punishment, The Idiot, The Possessed,* and *The Brothers Karamazov.* All of them are great **masterpieces.** He worked very hard. He usually worked late into the night, then slept until the early hours of the morning. He also worked quickly. Sometimes he worked on two books at a time—one in the morning, another in the afternoon.

⑪ Dostoyevsky was never a healthy man. He had very bad eyesight, which made it hard for him to work. He also had a serious brain disease called epilepsy. People with epilepsy shake violently and lose **consciousness.** Another illness caused him to lose consciousness and remain very still for a long time, as if he were dead. Because of this, Dostoyevsky had a terrible fear of being buried alive.

⑫ Dostoyevsky died at age 59 after years of illness. Thirty thousand people watched his coffin pass through the streets of Saint Petersburg. It was the largest funeral **procession** in Russian history. When he died, he was Russia's greatest writer. Now many believe he is one of the greatest writers in the world.

VOCABULARY

◆ MEANING

What is the best meaning of the underlined words? Circle the letter of the correct answer.

1. They were <u>sentenced</u> to death.
   - a. put on trial
   - b. tortured or killed
   - c. given a legal punishment

2. Fyodor Dostoyevsky was a very <u>complicated</u> person.
   a. unhappy
   b. difficult to understand
   c. intelligent and successful

3. Fyodor lost a lot of his money <u>gambling</u>.
   a. playing games to win money
   b. taking jobs that pay a low salary
   c. giving money to people that don't need it

4. It was the largest funeral <u>procession</u> in Russian history.
   a. large group of musicians
   b. ceremony with many speeches
   c. line of people or cars moving slowly

5. All of them are great <u>masterpieces</u>.
   a. things that are larger than everything around them
   b. works that are the best of their kind
   c. things that are very expensive

6. He was <u>conceited</u>.
   a. concerned only with money
   b. didn't want to help others
   c. had too high an opinion of himself

7. His illness caused him to lose <u>consciousness</u>.
   a. intelligence and creativity
   b. awareness of what is happening
   c. feeling of happiness

8. Dostoyevsky was very <u>relieved</u>, but this experience tortured him.
   a. surprised about something
   b. happy because something bad didn't happen
   c. nervous about the future

9. He was also a <u>literary</u> genius.
   a. related to math, science, and engineering
   b. related to Russian history
   c. related to books and plays

10. The prisoners were sentenced to four years of hard <u>labor</u> in a prison camp in Siberia.
    a. work done with the hands
    b. time completely alone in prison
    c. beatings and torture

◆ USE

Work with a partner and answer these questions. Use complete sentences.

1. How does a *conceited* person act?
2. When and where do you see *processions*?
3. What is your favorite *masterpiece* of art or literature?
4. What part of learning English is *complicated*?
5. When do people feel *relieved*?

◆ **EXTENSION: THE SUFFIXES -NESS AND -ITY**

Look at the sentences from the reading:

> People with epilepsy shake violently and lose **conscious<u>ness</u>.**

> He took **responsibil<u>ity</u>** for caring for his brother's family.

The suffixes -*ness* and -*ity* mean "quality of" or "state of being." When you add -*ness* or -*ity* to some adjectives, they become nouns.

(adjective)　　　　　　　　　(noun)
conscious + -*ness* = consciousness (state of being conscious)

(adjective)　　　　　　　　　(noun)
responsible + -*ity* = responsibility (quality of being responsible)

Add the correct suffix –*ness* or –*ity* to these adjectives. Then complete the sentences with the correct words. If you need help, check your dictionary.

Example: *sad<u>ness</u>*

equal _____　　weak _____

ill _____　　neat _____

serious _____　　popular _____

similar _____　　dark _____

1. Our lights went out at nine o'clock last night. The house was in total
   _____ for over an hour.

2. Everything is in its place in her apartment. _____ is very
   important to her.

3. He speaks and reads English well. His _____ is spelling. It's very
   bad.

4. The _____ of blue jeans around the world is unbelievable.

5. Many countries still do not have _____ between men and women.

6. There is some _____ between the two TV shows, but the one on
   Channel 5 is funnier.

7. Scientists are studying the _____ of the damage caused by the
   earthquake.

8. He was very weak and tired from his _____.

COMPREHENSION

◆ UNDERSTANDING MAIN IDEAS

Circle the letter of the best answer.

1. The main topic of paragraph 4 is that _____.
   a. Dostoyevsky's first novel made him famous, but also made him a difficult person
   b. Dostoyevsky published his first novel himself
   c. Dostoyevsky hated army life, so he left the army after just two years

2. Paragraph 6 is mostly about _____.
   a. why Dostoyevsky and the others were arrested and sentenced to die
   b. how Dostoyevsky was arrested and sentenced, then escaped death
   c. the conditions in the prison and his hard labor

3. The main topic of paragraph 8 is that Dostoyevsky _____.
   a. began to gamble to raise money for his family
   b. married and returned to Saint Petersburg to finish his book
   c. had problems with money, illness, and death in his family

4. Paragraph 11 is mainly about _____.
   a. what caused Dostoyevsky's illnesses
   b. why Dostoyevsky was afraid to be buried alive
   c. how Dostoyevsky's illnesses affected him

◆ REMEMBERING DETAILS

Reread the passage and complete the sentences.

1. Dostoyevsky was in debt because he lost money _____.

2. The publishers wanted Dostoyevsky to _____ to his novel.

3. Dostoyevsky's political group wanted the serfs _____.

4. When Dostoyevsky and the other prisoners were going to be shot, they wore

   _____ even though the weather was _____.

5. Dostoyevsky worked as a prisoner in Siberia for _____ years.

6. After his brother died, Dostoyevsky helped care for _____.

◆ ORDER OF EVENTS

Number the sentences 1–6 to show the correct order.

___ Dostoyevsky wrote *Crime and Punishment.*

___ Dostoyevsky went to college.

___ Dostoyevsky married Anna Snitkina.

___ Dostoyevsky was sentenced to death.

___ Dostoyevsky joined a secret political group.

___ Dostoyevsky's wife, brother, and close friend died.

The answers to these questions are not directly stated in the passage. Circle the letter of the best answer.

1. The passage concludes that _____.
   a. Dostoyevsky wanted to be a writer for most of his life
   b. Dostoyevsky only wanted to write about prison life
   c. Dostoyevsky was so depressed after being in prison that it was very difficult for him to write

2. The passage suggests that _____.
   a. Dostoyevsky didn't care about anyone except himself
   b. Dostoyevsky was a kind man who was misunderstood by others
   c. Dostoyevsky had many faults, but he tried to help people

3. The passage implies that _____.
   a. all of Dostoyevsky's life was painful and unhappy
   b. Dostoyevsky had many troubles, but he was a happy man who enjoyed his life
   c. Dostoyevsky's first marriage brought him the only happiness in his life

DISCUSSION

Discuss the answers to these questions with your classmates.

1. Dostoyevsky became conceited after he became famous. Do you think fame affects everyone in the same way?
2. Dostoyevsky lived in terrible conditions in prison. What do you think prison life should be like?
3. Dostoyevsky had a problem with gambling. Should gambling be legal? Why or why not?

WRITING

On a separate piece of paper, write a paragraph or more about someone who has had a positive or negative effect on your life.

Example: *The person who has had the most positive effect on my life is my mother. My mother always taught me to be honest and strong.*

UNIT 5
SARAH BERNHARDT
(1844–1923)

BEFORE YOU READ

Sarah Bernhardt was a famous actress. Many people thought she was one of the greatest actresses in history.

Discuss these questions with a partner.

1. Who are some famous actresses of the past?
2. Who are some famous actresses of the present?
3. Who is your favorite actress of all time? Why?

Now read about Sarah Bernhardt.

SARAH BERNHARDT

[1] Many people believe that Sarah Bernhardt was the greatest actress in the history of the theater. She fascinated audiences around the world. People **adored** her and called her "The **Divine** Sarah." Her performances were very **dramatic** and so was her life.

[2] Sarah was born in 1844 in a poor neighborhood in Paris. Her mother, Julie Bernard, was a beautiful woman who had many boyfriends. Sarah never knew her father. Julie loved to travel and there was no place in her life for Sarah. So, Sarah grew up feeling unwanted.

[3] Friends and family members helped to care for Sarah. Mostly she lived with her nurse in a small, dark room in a poor, dirty neighborhood. She was thin, pale, and sick-looking. She was also very unhappy. When Sarah was about five years old, she threw herself out a window when her aunt refused to take her home with her. Sarah was badly hurt and she couldn't walk. Her mother was forced to take care of her until she was well enough to go away to boarding school.

[4] Sarah had a bad temper and loved to break the rules. The boarding school didn't want her, so her mother sent her to a Catholic convent school where the teachers were nuns. Sarah needed to be disciplined and educated. This wasn't easy because Sarah had a lot of energy and **passion.** She tried to use her energy in a good way. She started studying to become a nun. This didn't work because Sarah was still very rebellious. In the end, the convent couldn't **handle** Sarah and the nuns asked her to leave. Sarah's family had to think of something else to do with their wild child.

[5] When Sarah was about 16, a friend of her mother's suggested that she study acting. Sarah wasn't sure about it, but everyone else thought it was a wonderful idea. She chose a scene to perform for the examination to enter the French government's acting school, the Paris Conservatoire. She studied very hard. When she began the scene, the judges stopped her. They wanted her to choose a boy to act in the scene with her. But Sarah had practiced alone, so she refused. The judges were shocked, but they offered to let Sarah perform something else. She chose to tell a story she knew. This was very unusual because the judges wanted her to act, not tell a story. But Sarah insisted. She told the story with such brilliance that she was accepted even before she finished.

[6] Sarah studied at the Conservatoire for several years and made her first stage appearance at the national theater company, the Comédie Française, when she was 17. It was the most **prestigious** theater in Europe. But Sarah's **debut** was a failure. When she heard what people thought about her, she swallowed poison and almost died. "Life is useless," she said to her friends. "I wanted to see what death was like." Sarah continued to act without much success. She finally left the company after she **slapped** the face of their oldest and most respected actress.

[7] Sarah Bernhardt had a terrible temper. But she also had charm, passion, and a strong personality. She had friends and boyfriends all over Europe. Around this time, she gave birth to her only child, Maurice. But like her mother, she didn't marry his father, who was a prince. Bernhardt wanted to be free to do whatever she wanted. She was 22 now and determined to succeed. She joined the

Odéon Theater and studied very hard for the next six years. She performed with all her energy and passion and became a well-respected actress.

⑧ In 1869, Bernhardt had her first great success. She acted in a play called *Le Passant* (*"The Passerby"*), which played for over 100 nights. She was on her way to a brilliant career. But the Franco-German War interrupted her life for a while. Paris was under attack. In 1870, Bernhardt organized a military hospital in the theater. After the war ended in 1871, the Odéon began to produce plays again, and she returned to acting. The audiences loved her and the critics went wild. The Comédie Française asked her to come back to them. She gave unforgettable performances. Her fans called her "The Divine Sarah."

⑨ People began to tell stories about Bernhardt. Some were true, some were not so true. They said she smoked cigars and acted like a man. Because she was thin and played male roles, some people said she was a boy dressed up in women's clothes. Sarah loved the **publicity** and lived a life as wild, exciting, and **bizarre** as the stories about her.

⑩ Sarah Bernhardt worked hard and didn't rest. Her doctors told her that if she didn't rest, she would die at a young age. She was always fascinated by death. No one played a death scene like Sarah Bernhardt. She liked to walk around in cemeteries. She always kept a special coffin and placed it beside her bed so it would be the first thing she saw when she woke up. Sometimes she slept in it. Sometimes she served tea to her friends on it. She brought the coffin with her wherever she went. Bernhardt was pretty wild, so it isn't surprising that she had a few wild pets, including a wildcat, two young lions, and a young tiger. She took them with her to the theater and kept them in her dressing room during her performances.

⑪ Sarah Bernhardt became the leading actress of the Comédie Française. When the company traveled to London, thousands of people came to see *her* and not the Comédie Française. After her last perfomance in the United States, 50,000 people came to the stage door to say goodbye to her. But the management didn't like her temper or her strange lifestyle. When the managers told her this, she left the company and formed her own. She called it the Sarah Bernhardt theater. She played many important parts. In fact, she was one of the first women to play Hamlet. By then she was 36 years old. She traveled around the world and became an international celebrity. There was no actor or actress in the world like Sarah Bernhardt.

⑫ Bernhardt was not like other actresses; age didn't hurt her career. She became more brilliant as she got older. It seemed that nothing could stop her. She worked 14 and 15 hours a day and played the most difficult roles. When she was 64 years old, she shocked audiences when she played 19-year-old Joan of Arc. Around this time, Bernhardt hurt her leg during a performance. The leg never healed properly, and she suffered with pain for many years. In 1915, her leg had to be cut off, so Sarah began to play her parts sitting in a wheelchair. The following year, during World War I, she still entertained the soldiers. When she was 79, she worked on a film for an American producer. But she was too ill to leave her house, so he filmed her in her living room. When she could no longer sit in a chair she said, "Film me in bed." Then Sarah Bernhardt died. She was buried in the coffin she always took with her.

VOCABULARY

◆ MEANING

Write the correct words in the blanks.

handle	publicity	debut	passion	adore
divine	slap	prestigious	dramatic	bizarre

1. _____ is a very strong and often uncontrollable feeling, especially of love, hate, or anger.

2. To _____ is to hit someone quickly with the flat part of the hand.

3. Something _____ is exciting and impressive.

4. To _____ something is to control it.

5. Something _____ is strange, peculiar, or odd.

6. The first time someone performs in public is a _____.

7. Something excellent that is almost godlike is _____.

8. The attention that someone or something famous gets is called

   _____.

9. To love and admire someone very much is to _____ that person.

10. Something _____ is respected and admired by many people.

◆ USE

Work with a partner and answer these questions. Use complete sentences.

1. What are some of the world's most *prestigious* universities?
2. What are some things that people have a lot of *passion* about?
3. When was the last time you had to *handle* a difficult person or situation?
4. Who gets a lot of *publicity*?
5. What was a recent *dramatic* event?

◆ EXTENSION: FOREIGN WORDS

Look at the sentence from the reading:

   But Sarah's **debut** was a failure.

Debut is a French word that has become a part of the English language. There are many words and expressions that we use in English that come from French and other languages.

Complete the sentences with the correct words. If you need help, check your dictionary.

gourmet   chic   encore   facade

vice versa   ego   patio   safari

1. They are a very happy couple. She loves him and _____.

2. The new restaurant is excellent. It serves _____ Italian food.

3. We saw many interesting animals when we went on a _____.

4. She always dresses elegantly in the latest fashion. She's so _____.

5. He thinks he's very important. He has a big _____.

6. The audience applauded so much that the pianist played an _____.

7. The weather is so beautiful tonight. Let's sit on the _____.

8. She puts on a happy _____, but she is really very sad.

COMPREHENSION

◆ UNDERSTANDING MAIN IDEAS

Circle the letter of the best answer.

1. Paragraph 3 is mostly about _____.
   a. how Sarah lived as a child
   b. the attitudes of family members toward Sarah
   c. Sarah's health as a child

2. The main topic of paragraph 8 is _____.
   a. what Bernhardt did during the war
   b. the Franco-German War
   c. the beginning of Bernhardt's great career

3. Paragraph 10 is mostly about Bernhardt's _____.
   a. poor health
   b. strange habits and interests
   c. ability to act out death scenes

4. The main topic of paragraph 12 is _____.
   a. that old age and illness didn't affect Bernhardt's brilliant career
   b. how Bernhardt shocked people with her performance as Joan of Arc
   c. how Bernhardt suffered with pain in her final years

◆ REMEMBERING DETAILS

Circle the letter of the best answer.

1. Sarah threw herself out a window because she _____.
   a. wanted to go to boarding school
   b. wanted to live with her aunt
   c. was trying to get her mother's attention

2. Sarah's family decided that she should study acting because _____.
   a. they didn't know what to do with her next
   b. Sarah showed great promise as an actress
   c. Sarah always wanted to be an actress

3. Sarah's examination to enter the Conservatoire was very unusual because she _____.
   a. told a story instead of acting a scene
   b. acted out a scene with a boy
   c. didn't choose the scene the judges had suggested

4. During the Franco-German War, Bernhardt _____.
   a. continued to act
   b. started her own theater company
   c. organized a military hospital

5. One of Bernhardt's strange activities was _____.
   a. sleeping in a coffin
   b. serving tea in a cemetery
   c. going on stage with wild animals

6. Bernhardt started her own company after the Comédie Française _____.
   a. refused to send her to the United States
   b. criticized the way she lived
   c. told her she was too old to act

◆ ORDER OF EVENTS

Number the sentences 1–6 to show the correct order.

___ The convent asked Bernhardt to leave.

___ Bernhardt worked on a film with an American producer.

___ Bernhardt became the leading actress of the Comédie Française.

___ Bernhardt failed in her stage debut.

___ Bernhardt played the role of Joan of Arc.

___ Bernhardt started her own theater company.

The answers to these questions are not directly stated in the passage. Circle the letter of the best answer.

1. The passage concludes that _____.
   a. Bernhardt's strange lifestyle almost destroyed her career
   b. Bernhardt's bizarre and emotional personality had a good effect on her career
   c. Bernhardt's happy and normal childhood helped her career

2. The passage suggests that _____.
   a. Bernhardt's acting career was the most important thing in the world to her
   b. Bernhardt wanted to change to please other people
   c. Bernhardt wanted to succeed but didn't like to work hard

3. The passage implies that _____.
   a. Bernhardt should have stopped acting as she got older
   b. Bernhardt was no longer a celebrity when she was older and sick
   c. most actresses of that time gave up their careers as they got older

DISCUSSION

Discuss the answers to these questions with your classmates.

1. Do you prefer theater, movies, or television? Why?
2. Would you like to be a famous actor or actress? Why or why not?
3. Many American actresses feel that "all the best parts go to younger actresses." Do you think this is true?

WRITING

On a separate piece of paper, write a paragraph or more about what kinds of things or people you like to have around you. Give your reasons.

Example: *I always love to have photographs around me. These photographs are of my family and friends.*

UNIT 6
NIKOLA TESLA
(1856–1943)

BEFORE YOU READ

Nikola Tesla was a great inventor who created the alternating current, or AC, electrical system as well as many other inventions.

Discuss these questions with a partner.

1. What great inventors of the past and present can you name?
2. What is the most important invention of the twentieth century?
3. What invention would you like to see in your lifetime?

Now read about Nikola Tesla.

NIKOLA TESLA

⊡ Nikola Tesla is one of the most important inventors in history. Tesla designed over 120 inventions. Most of them are still used today in one form or another. He invented **fluorescent** lights, sun-powered engines, robots, the first electric clock, and a very important machine part that is used in all radios and televisions. His most important invention was alternating current electricity, or AC. This electrical system is used in every home, factory, and office in the modern world. Yet most people do not even know who Nikola Tesla is.

② Nikola Tesla was born in 1856 in Smiljan, Croatia. Nikola was an unusual child. He had a photographic memory, so he remembered whole pages of books after he looked at them very quickly. He also liked to write poetry. When he was five, he built a waterwheel and he tried to fly in a homemade plane. That same year, Nikola's older brother died. People said Nikola accidentally pushed him down the stairs. After this, Nikola began to act strangely.

③ As a child, Nikola was often sick with mysterious illnesses that doctors couldn't cure. He also saw **flashes** of light when he got excited or when he was thinking hard about something. When Nikola started doing something, he couldn't stop. When he was eight, he became obsessed with reading books and often read all night without sleeping. Later, when he was a student at the University of Prague, he studied from three o'clock in the morning until eleven o'clock each night. For most of his life, Tesla slept for only two hours each night.

④ While Tesla was at the University of Prague, he thought of the idea to use an AC current in a motor. He **reversed** the direct current (DC) that comes from a battery. The alternating current was a better, stronger type of electricity. His professor said it couldn't be done, but Tesla did it. When Tesla's father died, he had to leave school and find a job. Tesla went to work for a telephone company in Budapest. But he couldn't stop thinking about his idea. Like everything else he did, he didn't stop until he solved the problem.

⑤ One day, Nikola Tesla had a **vision** of a whole new type of electric power system. Tesla went to work as an engineer for the Continental Edison Company. While he was there, he built the first model of his motor. But the people at the company weren't interested in it. Tesla decided to go to the United States to talk to the great inventor Thomas Edison. He arrived with only 14 cents in his pocket!

⑥ But Edison didn't like his idea one bit. After all, Edison was the inventor of the DC system of electricity. Edison gave Tesla a job, however. He gave him a project he thought was impossible. Tesla had to rework every power generator in New York City. Tesla started his day at 10:30 A.M. and stopped working at 5:00 A.M. the next morning. He did this seven days a week. Sometimes he worked for two or three days without stopping. When Tesla finished, Edison refused to pay him the $50,000 he had promised. After this, Edison and Nikola Tesla were enemies.

⑦ Nikola Tesla created the Tesla Electric Light Company and received 40 patents for AC equipment. Patents are legal papers that give a person the right to be the only one to make a new invention. Then he sold the patents to the head of Westinghouse Electric Company, George Westinghouse, for $1 million plus money from future sales. Now there was a war between Tesla and Edison to see which system, AC or DC, was the best. Thomas Edison tried to make people think Tesla's AC system was bad. He actually told the press that the AC system was dangerous, which wasn't true.

⑧ Meanwhile Nikola Tesla gave speeches around the country. He also invited the press to his laboratory for demonstrations so he could show that his inventions were safe. Once, he let one million volts of electricity pass through his body without using a wire. This caused a bulb to light in his hand. A few years later, Westinghouse used AC generators at Niagara Falls, a huge waterfall on the U.S.-Canadian border, to send electric power 22 miles away to the city of Buffalo. This made Nikola Tesla world famous.

⑨ Nikola Tesla was a tall, handsome man who spoke eight languages. He was also very eccentric. He dressed in the best suits and hats and always carried a silk handkerchief. He always wore his silk shirt, tie, and gloves only once, then threw them away. He lived in hotels, and only stayed in rooms with numbers that could be divided by three. There were always 18 napkins at his table when he ate. He used them to clean and polish the silverware and crystal before each meal. He almost always ate his meals alone, and he never ate with a woman. Tesla always calculated the exact mathematical measurement of the soup, coffee, and every portion of food **prior to** eating it. Another interesting thing about Tesla was that he had many **psychic** experiences. He knew about things before they happened. Tesla knew when his sister was seriously ill and when his mother died. Once after a party, he told his guests not to take a certain train. That same night, the train crashed and injured many people.

⑩ Tesla was incredibly brilliant, which made him a great success but also helped to destroy him. He wanted to be perfect and pushed himself so much that he had terrible mental problems. Sometimes he concentrated so hard that he saw and heard nothing around him. The hotel workers sometimes cleaned his room around him without seeing him move a muscle.

⑪ Tesla was never **motivated** by money. At one point, Westinghouse told Tesla that he couldn't pay him the $12 million he owed him for sales of Tesla's product. Tesla said Westinghouse was his friend and that he shouldn't worry about paying him. Tesla then tore up his contract. Unfortunately, later he didn't have the money to research and build his other inventions. In 1895, a fire destroyed Tesla's laboratory and all of his research, including his work on radio communications, X-rays, and a system to send and receive sound without using wires, which we now call broadcasting.

⑫ Tesla continued his work and **came up with** the idea of an engine that uses the sun's power. After his work with solar power, he became interested in the idea of controlling the weather. He **set up** a laboratory in Colorado where he developed the Tesla coil, which is a machine part used in radios and televisions. He also created lightning when he tried to **transmit** electrical energy without wires. Some of these ideas seemed crazy, but many of them led to inventions we now use every day.

⑬ As the years went by, Tesla didn't have the money to finish his projects and people heard less and less about him. He spent much of his time sitting in a park and feeding birds. In 1915, he refused to share the Nobel Prize with Thomas Edison and many people lost respect for him. He liked to be alone and he refused to write down his work or share his ideas with other scientists.

⑭ Tesla died a poor man at the age of 87. He was a serious scientist, who was interested only in seeing his inventions work and be used. He is remembered as a creative genius and a very important figure in the field of electrical science.

VOCABULARY

◆ MEANING

Match the words with their meanings.

___ 1. vision	a. having strange experiences that cannot be explained
___ 2. flash	
___ 3. psychic	b. to be the reason that someone wants to do something
___ 4. fluorescent	
___ 5. motivate	c. sudden, quick, bright light
___ 6. transmit	d. before
___ 7. reverse	e. to change something so that it goes the other way
___ 8. prior to	f. idea or dream
___ 9. come up with	g. to start something new
___10. set up	h. very bright, glowing, cool light
	i. to think of
	j. to send out or carry across

◆ USE

Work with a partner and answer these questions. Use complete sentences.

1. Where are *fluorescent* lights used?
2. What kinds of things might be needed to *set up* a classroom?
3. What are some things that people with *psychic* abilities can do?
4. Where might you see *flashes* of light?
5. What are some things that *motivate* people to work hard?

◆ EXTENSION: PHRASAL VERBS

Look at the sentence from the reading:

> He **set up** a laboratory in Colorado.

Set up is a phrasal verb. Phrasal verbs are verbs that are made up of a verb plus one or more particles (adverbs or prepositions).

Match the phrasal verbs with their meanings.

_f_ 1. put off		a. to have a friendly relationship with someone
_e_ 2. show up		b. to put your name on a list to join something
_h_ 3. find out		c. to stop all work at a business
_a_ 4. get along		d. to make something start working
_d_ 5. turn on		e. to arrive someplace
_g_ 6. run out		f. to delay doing something
_b_ 7. sign up		g. to use all of something
_c_ 8. close down		h. to learn the facts about something

Use each phrasal verb in a sentence. Then add three of your own phrasal verbs and use each in a sentence.

COMPREHENSION

◆ UNDERSTANDING MAIN IDEAS

Circle the letter of the best answer.

1. The main topic of paragraph 1 is _____.
   a. the fact that Tesla invented many things, but is not well-known
   b. Tesla's machine part that is used in all radios and televisions
   c. the importance of the AC electrical system

2. Paragraph 9 is mainly about the fact that _____.
   a. Tesla was brilliant but he didn't have many friends
   b. Tesla had unusual eating habits
   c. Tesla had strange habits and experiences

3. The main topic of paragraph 11 is _____.
   a. some unfortunate incidents that affected Tesla's research and work
   b. that Tesla didn't want money but needed it for research
   c. the friendship between Tesla and Westinghouse

4. Paragraph 13 is mostly about _____.
   a. why people lost respect for Tesla
   b. how Tesla behaved as he got older
   c. why Tesla didn't finish his projects

◆ REMEMBERING DETAILS

Circle the letter of the best answer.

1. When Tesla told his professor about his idea for his new motor, the professor _____.
   a. helped Tesla build the first model
   b. told Tesla to go see Thomas Edison
   c. said it couldn't be done

2. Edison and Tesla became enemies when _____.
   a. Tesla didn't tell Edison about his new motor
   b. Edison gave Tesla an impossible project
   c. Edison refused to pay Tesla the money he promised

3. Tesla sold his patents to _____.
   a. Thomas Edison
   b. George Westinghouse
   c. a telephone company in Budapest

4. To prove that his AC system was safe, Tesla _____.
   a. set up his generators at Niagara Falls
   b. made a bulb light up in his hand
   c. made lightning

5. Tesla was very interested in _____.
   a. building weapons
   b. controlling the weather
   c. using wires to transmit electric energy

6. Many people lost respect for Tesla when he refused to _____.
   a. share the Nobel Prize
   b. work in the same laboratory with Thomas Edison
   c. finish his projects

◆ ORDER OF EVENTS

Number the sentences 1–6 to show the correct order.

_6_ Tesla refused to share the Nobel Prize with Thomas Edison.

_3_ Tesla created the Tesla Electric Company.

_2_ Tesla decided to go to the United States.

_1_ Tesla went to the University of Prague.

_4_ A fire destroyed Tesla's laboratory.

_5_ Tesla set up a laboratory in Colorado.

The answers to these questions are not directly stated in the passage. Circle the letter of the best answer.

1. The passage implies that Edison _____.
   a. didn't want Tesla to be more famous than he was
   b. wanted to be friends with Tesla
   c. helped Tesla improve his AC system

2. The passage suggests that _____.
   a. Tesla wished he hadn't torn up his contract
   b. Tesla's love of money caused him to fail in the end
   c. Tesla's eccentric ways sometimes caused problems

3. The passage concludes that Tesla _____.
   a. was as brilliant in business as he was in science
   b. was happy with his life in his old age
   c. might be more famous if he had worked better with others

DISCUSSION

Discuss the answers to these questions with your classmates.

1. Tesla didn't care at all about money. Some people care too much about money. How important is money in your life?
2. In school or work, do you prefer to work alone or in a group? Explain.
3. Tesla said he had psychic experiences, where he knew something was going to happen before it did. Do you believe that some people have psychic experiences? Have you ever had one?

WRITING

On a separate piece of paper, write about the good and bad points of an important invention.

Example: *A popular invention today is the cell phone. This invention has many good points and some bad points.*

UNIT 7

SIGMUND FREUD
(1856–1939)

BEFORE YOU READ

Sigmund Freud developed new ways to treat mentally ill patients and helped the world to understand the human mind.

Discuss these questions with a partner.

1. What causes people to have mental problems?
2. How do you think mental problems were treated 100 years ago?
3. How are mental problems treated today?

Now read about Sigmund Freud.

SIGMUND FREUD

[1] Many people believe that Sigmund Freud's work marked the beginning of modern psychology. He developed new ways to study the human personality. Some people disagreed with his ideas, and others thought he was a genius.

[2] Sigmund Freud was born in 1856 in Moravia, which is now the Czech Republic. His family moved to Vienna when Sigmund was four years old. He was the oldest of his mother's eight children and her favorite. Sigmund loved to read and he was always at the top of his class. He had no interest in sports or outdoor activities, except walking. The family apartment had only four bedrooms, but Sigmund's mother gave him his own room so he could study in peace. He rarely joined the family for meals. Instead he ate alone in his room, surrounded by his favorite books.

[3] Sigmund Freud first thought about studying law, but then he decided to study medicine. He enrolled at the University of Vienna in 1873. His early days at the university were difficult because some of his classmates **discriminated against** him because he was Jewish. This made Freud more determined than ever to do his best. He loved working in the laboratory and studying the scientific side of medicine rather than helping patients. In fact, he stayed in school for seven years instead of the usual five because he spent so much time working in the laboratory of a famous professor. Freud expected to become the professor's assistant, but unfortunately, he was discriminated against again.

[4] Freud received his medical degree in 1881. For the next few years he continued his laboratory work. Meanwhile, he fell in love and became engaged to a young woman named Martha Bernays. Freud didn't earn a lot of money working in the laboratory, so he took a job at the General Hospital of Vienna. He worked in several departments, including the **psychiatry** department, where he studied the human nervous system and mental illnesses. Freud became fascinated by the human mind. After several months, he went to a clinic in Paris to study with a leading specialist in the field. After four months, he realized how much he missed Martha, and he returned to Vienna. They got married a few weeks later and went on to have a family of six children.

[5] After his marriage, Freud opened his own psychiatry **practice.** He worked with patients who were very depressed or behaved in strange ways. At first he used **hypnosis, a technique** he had studied in Paris. Under hypnosis, patients could sometimes remember experiences that caused their problems. Many doctors at the time disagreed with the use of hypnosis, but Freud kept trying. Some patients were helped by this and others were not, so he kept looking for more ways to understand the human mind.

[6] Around this time, Freud started to treat patients in a new way, called "psychoanalysis." Psychoanalysis uses different techniques to help people. One technique that Freud used was to let his patients talk about whatever they wanted, sometimes for hours at a time. At first they couldn't remember what made them depressed or upset. But after a while, their memories came back. After talking about their experiences and understanding the cause of their troubles, many patients felt much better. Freud also talked about the

unconscious mind as the cause of mental and emotional problems. He believed that often people aren't aware of the things that upset them. Related to this is Freud's work with dreams. Freud believed that strange behavior was often connected to past worries, fears, and desires, which often appear in our dreams. By getting patients to remember their dreams, he could understand what upset them. Then he helped them to overcome their problems. In 1910, Freud wrote a book called *The Interpretation of Dreams,* which explained what dreams mean. Many people were shocked and angered by the ideas in his book. They thought that dreams had nothing to do with people's problems.

7 When news of Freud's work began to spread, people laughed at him and called him a **fraud.** Freud was very stubborn in his professional life. He ignored the people who **criticized** him and continued his work. He published study after study. Some countries banned his books and many religious groups **condemned** him. But several of Vienna's younger doctors and a group of respected psychiatrists from around the world admired him. After a while, some of Freud's most famous admirers began to disagree with his ideas. They started using their own techniques and Freud never forgave them. Freud wouldn't listen to anyone's ideas and arguments but his own.

8 In his personal life, Freud was a loving father and husband. He loved to take his children for walks in the country, where they picked flowers and mushrooms. He also liked to play card games every week with his friends. Freud was interested in archaeology and he collected Egyptian and Greek antiques. He didn't like the telephone and rarely listened to the radio. Freud hated chicken and the vegetable cauliflower and refused to sit at a table if these foods were served. He was also afraid of open spaces and trains. Freud was of average height and had black hair and a short beard. He liked to wear nice suits with a black tie and black hat. He also smoked 20 cigars a day. Unfortunately, Freud had health problems. He had cancer of the mouth and had over 30 surgeries. During one surgery, doctors had to remove part of his tongue and it was hard for him to speak.

9 In 1938, the German army invaded Austria. World War II was beginning, and life became terrible for millions of Jews, including Sigmund Freud. The army burnt many of his books in public. They also destroyed the publishing company that printed them. One day as he was coming home from the hospital, the German secret police took him. They also took his money, his house, and his land. Freud needed a **miracle** to save his life now. The miracle came when U.S. President Franklin D. Roosevelt asked the German army to set him free. They agreed to let Freud leave Austria but they wanted 20,000 pounds sterling (approximately $32,000). A Greek princess who was once a patient of Freud's paid the money. However, Freud had to sign a paper saying that he was treated well by the German army. Freud signed the paper and added in his own handwriting, "I can most warmly recommend the Gestapo to anyone." On June 4, 1938, Freud and his family moved to a town near London. Fifteen months later, in September 1939, Freud died at the age of 83.

VOCABULARY

◆ MEANING

Match the words with their meanings.

___ 1. fraud ___ 2. psychiatry ___ 3. condemn ___ 4. discriminate against ___ 5. practice ___ 6. unconscious ___ 7. criticize ___ 8. miracle ___ 9. hypnosis ___10. technique	a. to treat someone you think is different in an unfair way b. person who lies and claims to be something he or she is not c. special way of doing some special activity or work d. to express very strong disapproval of someone or something e. sleeplike state in which a person's thoughts or actions can be controlled by someone else f. to say what is wrong with something g. part of the mind where there are thoughts and feelings people don't realize they have h. study and treatment of mental illness i. business created by a doctor or lawyer j. an amazing or remarkable thing

◆ USE

Work with a partner and answer these questions. Use complete sentences.

1. What are some *frauds* that you have heard about?
2. Why is *psychiatry* an important area of study?
3. Do you find it hard to *criticize* people?
4. Would you like to go under *hypnosis*?
5. Why do some people *discriminate against* others?

◆ EXTENSION: ADJECTIVES TO DESCRIBE FEELINGS

Look at the sentence from the reading:

> He worked with patients who were very **depressed** or behaved in strange ways.

Depressed is an adjective that describes a feeling. There are many adjectives to describe feelings.

Put each of the adjectives in the correct column according to the feeling it describes. If you need help, check your dictionary.

depressed	infuriating	miserable	startled
annoyed	delighted	terrified	cheerful

HAPPY	*SAD*	*ANGRY*	*SCARED*
_____	_____	_____	_____
_____	_____	_____	_____

Use each word in a sentence.

COMPREHENSION

◆ UNDERSTANDING MAIN IDEAS

Circle the letter of the best answer.

1. The main topic of paragraph 3 is that Freud _____.
   a. was treated badly at the university
   b. became interested in laboratory and scientific work at the university
   c. spent more years at the university than most other students

2. Paragraph 6 is mostly about _____.
   a. how Freud used psychoanalysis to treat his patients
   b. why Freud's patients were depressed and upset
   c. how memories played an important part in the lives of Freud's patients

3. The main topic of paragraph 8 is Freud's _____.
   a. personal habits and interests
   b. strange behavior and fears
   c. relationship with his children

4. Paragraph 9 is mostly about _____.
   a. how Freud's cancer affected the last years of his life and led to his death
   b. how Freud was treated badly by the German army and finally escaped
   c. why the German army tried to destroy Freud and his work

◆ REMEMBERING DETAILS

Circle the letter of the best answer.

1. Freud took seven years to get his medical degree because _____.
   a. he went to law school first
   b. he spent a lot of time in laboratories
   c. school was difficult for him

2. Freud tried to get his patients to _____.
   a. forget about the bad things that happened to them
   b. remember their past experiences
   c. sleep longer so they could have more dreams

3. When people heard Freud's first ideas about the unconscious mind they
_____.

    a. ignored him   b. praised him   c. laughed at him

4. Freud believed that people's dreams _____.

    a. helped them to   b. caused them to   c. made them upset
       understand their   behave strangely   and angry
       hidden fears

5. Freud didn't like _____.

    a. open spaces   b. playing cards   c. his children

6. After the German army freed Freud, he moved to _____.

    a. the United States   b. England   c. Greece

◆ ORDER OF EVENTS

Number the sentences 1–6 to show the correct order.

____ Freud married Martha Bernays.

____ Freud went to a clinic in Paris to study.

____ Freud started to use psychoanalysis.

____ Freud wrote *The Interpretation of Dreams.*

____ Freud received his medical degree.

____ Freud opened his own psychiatry practice.

◆ MAKING INFERENCES

The answers to these questions are not directly stated in the passage. Circle the letter of the best answer.

1. The passage suggests that Freud _____.
    a. always believed his ideas were both important and correct
    b. was often upset by people's opinions of his work
    c. didn't always believe in himself, and allowed others to influence his work

2. The passage implies that Freud _____.
    a. was happy only when he was working
    b. was happy when he spent time with family and friends
    c. was a difficult and bitter man who had more enemies than friends

3. The passage concludes that _____.
    a. Freud's new ideas about human behavior made many people angry and upset
    b. in the late 1800s, no one thought Freud's ideas made any sense
    c. Freud's work was important in his time but isn't important today

DISCUSSION

Discuss the answers to these questions with your classmates.

1. Do you think psychoanalysis is helpful? Why?
2. Do you think dreams tell us something about ourselves? Explain.
3. How have attitudes toward mental problems changed over the years?

WRITING

On a separate piece of paper, write about a problem that a person you know has had.

Example: *My father has a problem with his new boss at work. My father has worked in this company for 20 years, but the new boss is young and does not like older people in the company.*

UNIT 8

PANDITA RAMABAI
(1858–1922)

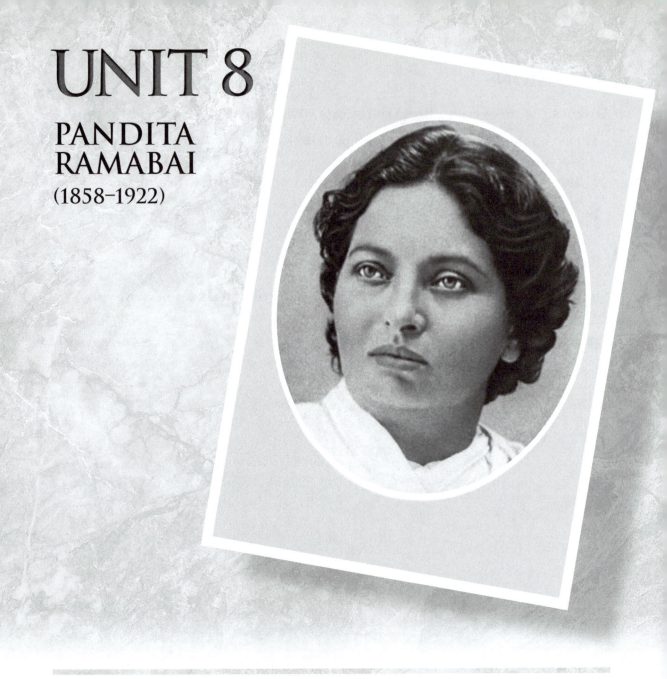

BEFORE YOU READ

Pandita Ramabai was famous for the work she did to help and protect the women of India.

Discuss these questions with a partner.

1. Who are some women who spent their lives helping others?
2. In what countries today do women not have equal rights?
3. In your country, do women have equal rights in careers? Education? Politics?

Now read about Pandita Ramabai.

PANDITA RAMABAI

[1] Pandita Ramabai is considered by many to be one of India's greatest **humanitarians.** She spent her life trying to improve the lives of Indian women. In the 1800s, arranged marriages were very common. In many cases, girls as young as nine years old were forced to marry older men that they did not know. When these men died, many of the girls became widows while they were still children. Young widows had very unhappy lives. Many Indians believed that these women were being punished for the sins of their past lives. A widow who had a son suffered a little less, since boys were more valuable than girls. A widow without a son, however, was treated like a criminal. Her husband's family put her in a dark corner of their home and only gave her one meal a day. They beat her and forced her to do all of the work around the house. Many of these young widows committed suicide rather than face a life of misery. Pandita Ramabai took the first steps to help these poor young women. In 1888, she opened the first **shelter** for child widows in India.

[2] Pandita Ramabai was born Ramabai Dongre in 1858. Ramabai's family was part of India's highest social **class.** Her father, Ananta Dongre, was 44 years old when his first wife died. One day he met a man while he was bathing in a river. The man offered him his nine-year-old daughter. Ananta married her and took her to his home. Ananta was different from many of the men in India at that time. He was an educated man with very modern ideas. His family was shocked when he began to educate his young wife. Everyone was against him. So Ananta took his new wife to southern India. He built a house near a Hindu **shrine** that **pilgrims** often visited. Ramabai was born soon after they moved.

[3] Ananta Dongre spent all of his money helping the pilgrims. Eventually, there was nothing left. So the Dongres, including six-month-old Ramabai, joined the pilgrims who traveled around India visiting the shrines and temples. Most of these people were very, very poor. Ananta was able to earn money by giving public readings of the sacred Sanskrit texts and translating them into different **dialects.** In return, people gave him a little bit of money, some rice, or a place to sleep. Still, the family often went hungry and had to sleep outside or in public shelters. Ramabai and her sister and brother were well educated by their parents. By the time Ramabai was 15, she could speak seven Indian dialects and **recite** 23,000 sacred verses from memory.

[4] In 1874, India suffered a terrible **famine.** Ramabai's parents and her sister died of starvation. Ramabai and her brother survived and continued to live as pilgrims. Like their father, they earned money to support themselves by reading sacred texts. Over the next few years, they walked for more than 4,000 miles. They had little or no food, no shelter, and no proper clothing. In 1878, Ramabai and her brother went to live in Calcutta. There, they read the Sanskrit writings to large groups of people. It was very unusual for a woman to read and write, so Ramabai became famous. They began to meet with important, well-educated people from other religions and classes. Calcutta University honored Ramabai with the title of "Pandita," which means "Learned Lady."

[5] When Ramabai was 22, her brother died. His death put Ramabai in a very difficult position. At that time, Indian women were completely **dependent** on male relatives. A woman could not have a

job, a home, or a life of her own. A young lawyer named Bipin Bihari Medhavi offered to marry Ramabai. However, he was from a lower social class than Ramabai. Both of their families rejected them because a Hindu could not speak to family members who married out of their class. But Ramabai and Bipin didn't care. They loved each other and they believed in the same ideas. They married in 1880 and moved to Poona.

6 Less than two years later, Bipin became sick with a very serious stomach disease. When he died, Ramabai was again in a very difficult situation. She had married outside her class and was now a widow with a baby girl. Neither her family nor her husband's family wanted to help her. Ramabai and her daughter would be out in the streets to live a life of poverty. Her only hope was to get help from a young female cousin, Anandibai Joshee. Anandibai was also an intelligent and independent woman. She later became the first Hindu woman to become a doctor. Anandibai planned to go to the United States to study. She suggested that Ramabai leave India too.

7 Ramabai went to the Christian missionaries at Poona and asked them for help. They agreed to send her to England and to pay for her education. In 1883, Ramabai and her daughter arrived in England. There, the Sisters of Saint Mary's gave her English lessons and also got her a job teaching Sanskrit. In addition, they showed her their women's shelter in London. Seeing the shelter gave Ramabai ideas for opening up her own shelter for Indian women. During this time, Ramabai also converted to become Christian.

8 In 1886, Ramabai went to the United States for her cousin Anandibai's graduation from medical school. She met many interesting women there. They encouraged her to stay in America to study and prepare for her return to India. For the next three years, Ramabai studied teaching methods in American schools. She also wrote a book, *The High-Caste Indian Woman.* It was the first book to talk about how the class system affected the lives of Indian women.

9 Ramabai became famous because of her book. In 1887, she and a group of wealthy Americans started the American Ramabai Association. With their money, Ramabai returned to India in November 1888 to start a school and shelter for child widows in Bombay. Five years later, she moved the school and shelter to Poona, and bought a large farm in nearby Kedgaon. There she established a Christian home and industrial school. She fed and clothed many girls and women and cared for their children. She also taught them to become teachers and nurses. She trained others to make clothes and shoes, and to do other work with their hands. Others worked on the farm and helped provide the school with food and water.

10 During the famine of 1896, Ramabai helped hundreds of young women. Three years later, she helped almost 2,000 people during another famine. Over the years, her schools and shelters gave hundreds of women a chance to have a new life. Pandita Ramabai died in 1922. Her determination to help the women of India will never be forgotten.

VOCABULARY

◆ MEANING

What is the best meaning of the underlined words? Circle the letter of the correct answer.

1. Ramabai's family was part of India's highest social <u>class</u>.
   - a. a group of people that live near each other
   - b. a group of people that have a similar way of life
   - c. a group of people that are part of the same religion

2. In 1874, India suffered a <u>famine</u>.
   - a. many bad storms over a long period of time
   - b. terrible diseases and illness
   - c. a time when many people have very little food

3. Ramabai opened the first <u>shelter</u> for child widows.
   - a. place that protects people from danger
   - b. area where everyone must remain quiet
   - c. school where people learn new skills

4. Indian women were <u>dependent</u> on male relatives.
   - a. needed someone for help or support
   - b. worked for someone for little pay
   - c. were afraid of someone

5. Pandita Ramabai was one of India's greatest <u>humanitarians</u>.
   - a. people who travel around the world
   - b. people who work to help others
   - c. people with money and power

6. Ramabai's father translated the sacred Sanskrit texts into many <u>dialects</u>.
   - a. different languages
   - b. different ways of writing the alphabet
   - c. different forms of the same language

7. Ramabai could <u>recite</u> sacred verses.
   - a. read by herself
   - b. write down word for word
   - c. say aloud from memory

8. Ananta built a house near a Hindu <u>shrine</u>.
   - a. home for religious people
   - b. place that people visit to pray
   - c. outdoor area where people meet

9. Both of their families <u>rejected</u> them.
   - a. would not accept
   - b. talked about
   - c. were afraid of

10. Many <u>pilgrims</u> visited the shrine.
    - a. people who pray in a special religious building
    - b. people who travel to religious places
    - c. people who work for the sick and poor

◆ USE

Work with a partner and answer these questions. Use complete sentences.

1. What are some causes of *famines*?
2. Who needs *shelters*?
3. What can you *recite*?
4. Who are you sometimes *dependent* on?
5. Who is a great *humanitarian*?
6. Do you know different *dialects* of your language?

◆ EXTENSION: THE SUFFIXES −IAN AND −IST

Look at the sentence from the reading:

Pandita Ramabai is considered by many to be one of India's greatest **humanitarians.**

The suffix −*ian* is for nouns that describe or refer to a person. The suffix −*ist* is also used to describe a person.

    (noun)   (noun)
humanity + −*ian* = humanitarian (person who cares about humanity)

(noun)   (noun)
piano + −*ist* = pianist (person who plays the piano)

Add the correct suffix −*ian* or −*ist* to these nouns. Make changes in the spelling where necessary. If you need help, check your dictionary.

Examples: *cartoon* *cartoonist*
             politics *politician*

1. history   _____
2. beauty   _____
3. psychiatry   _____
4. economics   _____
5. Buddha   _____
6. electricity   _____
7. chemistry   _____

Add three of your own words with −*ian* or −*ist*. Use each word in a sentence.

COMPREHENSION

◆ UNDERSTANDING MAIN IDEAS

Circle the letter of the best answer.

1. Paragraph 1 is mainly about _____.
   a. Hindu religious beliefs
   b. the treatment of Indian widows
   c. Pandita Ramabai's humanitarian work

2. The main topic of paragraph 3 is _____.
   a. Ramabai's education and abilities
   b. how Ramabai and her family lived as pilgrims
   c. how Ramabai's father lost his money

3. Paragraph 4 is mostly about _____.
   a. what happened after the famine
   b. how Ramabai became famous
   c. where Ramabai and her brother lived after the famine

4. The main topic of paragraph 9 is _____.
   a. how Ramabai helped women when she opened her schools and shelters
   b. how Americans started an association to help Ramabai return to India
   c. that Ramabai wrote a book that made her famous

◆ REMEMBERING DETAILS

Reread the passage and answer the questions.

1. How was a young Indian widow treated when she didn't have a son?
2. Why did Ananta Dongre's family refuse to speak to him?
3. How did Ananta Dongre use up all his money?
4. What could Ramabai do by the age of fifteen?
5. How did Ramabai and her brother support themselves while they were pilgrims?
6. Why was Ramabai in a very difficult situation after her husband died?

◆ ORDER OF EVENTS

Number the sentences 1–6 to show the correct order.

___ Ramabai went to the United States.

___ Calcutta University gave Ramabai the title "Pandita."

___ Ramabai's brother died.

___ Ramabai married Bipin Bihari Medhavi.

___ Ramabai wrote *The High-Caste Indian Woman*.

___ Ramabai established a Christian home and industrial school.

The answers to these questions are not directly stated in the passage. Circle the letter of the best answer.

1. The passage concludes that in nineteenth-century India _____.
   a. children were not loved and respected
   b. a male child had more worth than a female child
   c. people liked to have large families

2. The passage implies that _____.
   a. only some males in India were educated
   b. all males in India were educated
   c. all females born into the high classes were educated

3. The passage suggests that nineteenth-century Indian women _____.
   a. did not respect men
   b. controlled the home and family
   c. did not have rights or opportunities

DISCUSSION

Discuss the answers to these questions with your classmates.

1. How have the lives of most women changed in the past 100 years?
2. What do you think about arranged marriages? Explain.
3. Is it easy for a person to change social classes? Explain.

WRITING

On a separate piece of paper, write about the position of women in your home country today.

Example: *In my country, there are two positions for women. One is the traditional housewife who takes care of the house and children and covers her body and head in the Moslem way when she goes out. The other is the modern woman who is educated, has a job, and wears Western clothes.*

UNIT 9
MATTHEW HENSON
(1866–1955)

BEFORE YOU READ

Matthew Henson was an important African American explorer and the first person ever to reach the North Pole.

Discuss these questions with a partner.

1. What famous explorers can you name? What did these people discover?
2. What characteristics should an explorer have?
3. Who is a modern-day explorer?

Now read about Matthew Henson.

MATTHEW HENSON

[1] The North Pole is a very difficult place to get to. In the 1800s, many people tried, and failed, to reach the North Pole. But Matthew Henson was determined to succeed. He was part of the North Pole **expeditions** of Commander Robert E. Peary. Going to the North Pole was a very long journey. Day after day, Peary and his team traveled in unbearable conditions. Temperatures dropped as low as 60 degrees below zero. They traveled 18 to 20 hours a day and fought the cold, the wind, and the snow. The first six times they made the trip, they failed. The seventh time they reached their **goal**. Matthew Henson was the first to arrive at the North Pole. Commander Peary followed him, put the American flag in the ground, and then took the **credit** for himself.

[2] Matthew Henson was born in 1866 in Charles County, Maryland. His parents died when he was very young. Matthew went to live with an uncle in Washington, D.C. He went to school once in a while, but most of the time he washed dishes and served customers at a local restaurant. His favorite customer was a sailor. Matthew loved to listen to stories about his exciting life at sea.

[3] At age 12, Henson decided to try life as a sailor. He ran away from home and walked all the way to Baltimore, Maryland. It was a forty-mile trip! Then he got a job on a ship. The captain of the ship liked Henson very much and treated him almost like a son. He taught him to read and write and trained him to **navigate** a ship. For six years, Matthew sailed across the Atlantic and Pacific Oceans, into the China and Baltic seas, and through the Straits of Magellan at the tip of South America. He visited China, Africa, and many other faraway places. When the captain died, Henson returned to the United States. He got a job in a clothing store in Washington, D. C. This was very boring compared to sailing around the world. Soon Henson **longed for** something more exciting. He started thinking about going away again and having more adventures. Less than two years later, his dream came true.

[4] One day in 1887, a naval officer and explorer named Robert E. Peary walked into the store. He wanted to buy clothes for his expedition to Nicaragua. Henson told Peary about his navigating skills and experiences as a sailor. Peary was very impressed with Henson's knowledge and experience. He invited him to join the expedition as his personal assistant.

[5] Henson spent the next 20 years exploring with Commander Peary. He quickly became a very valuable part of the team. After the Nicaragua expedition, all their expeditions were to the North Pole. Robert Peary wanted to be the first man to reach the North Pole. Many people had tried, but none had succeeded. Henson soon began to share Peary's dream. He learned to speak the Eskimo language, to build and drive dog sleds, and to make special equipment they needed. Over the years, they made seven expeditions to the North Pole. Six times they had to turn back because of ice storms and freezing temperatures. They traveled in the cruelest conditions. Sometimes they were just a few hundred miles from their destination when they had to stop.

[6] In 1908, Peary, Henson, and their team left Greenland for their final expedition. The North Pole was nearly 500 miles away. They had six dog teams with them. Peary **assigned** Henson to the first dog sled.

Peary said, "He is a better dog driver than any man living except some of the best Eskimo hunters. I couldn't get along without him."

⑦ They traveled for almost 20 hours a day in **bitter** conditions. They had to keep stopping and waiting for the sea to freeze so they could walk on it. They couldn't carry food for more than 50 days, so they had to travel as far as they could as quickly as possible. During the last part of the expedition, Henson moved out front. He walked 35 miles on the first day. Peary followed behind, moving slower because he had lost several toes when they had frozen during another trip.

⑧ On the morning of April 6, 1909, Matthew Henson arrived at the North Pole. He waited for Peary to arrive to **confirm** his calculations that they were at the right place. It took the team about 30 hours to make all their observations and studies. Finally, Peary put the American flag in the ground and packed up their equipment for the long and difficult trip home.

⑨ Peary was very upset that Henson arrived at the North Pole before he did. He refused to shake Henson's hand when Henson tried to congratulate him. On the way home, Peary was unfriendly and told Henson not to speak publicly about their adventures when they returned. When they got home, Peary took all the credit for reaching the North Pole. He never mentioned Henson. Peary was honored as a hero, while Henson was ignored.

⑩ Henson kept silent for 12 years. While Peary won awards and gave speeches around the world, Henson worked at whatever job he could get. He even had a job parking cars! In 1912, Henson wrote a book called *A Negro Explorer at the North Pole*. But few people read it. People didn't think that an African American man could be a famous explorer. Stories about Peary's expeditions only mentioned Henson as being Peary's servant. This was far from the truth, because Henson's knowledge and skills were **crucial** to Peary's success. Finally, Henson's friends told President William Howard Taft about his accomplishments. Taft recommended Henson for a job at the U.S. Customs House in New York City.

⑪ Eventually, Henson started to give lectures around the country. People began to know who he was and to recognize him as an important explorer. In 1937, he was elected to the prestigious Explorers Club. In 1945, he received the Congressional Medal of Honor, 36 years after his journey to the North Pole. In 1947, he and another writer wrote a book titled *Dark Companion*. All this helped bring more attention to Henson's remarkable achievements.

⑫ Matthew Henson died in 1955. His family wanted him to be buried in Arlington National Cemetery where many important Americans are buried, including Robert Peary. But the government refused because Henson was never in the military. Six years after Henson's death, the state of Maryland put a **marker** with his name at the State House at Annapolis. It honored him as co-discoverer of the North Pole. Finally, in 1988, his body was buried with full honors next to Robert Peary at Arlington National Cemetery.

VOCABULARY

◆ MEANING

Write the correct words or expressions in the blanks.

navigate	crucial	bitter	expedition	confirm
goal	marker	assigned	long for	credit

1. Something that you hope to do in the future is a _____.

2. An _____ is a long trip people take, often to unusual or dangerous places.

3. When you give people praise or approval for doing something good, you give them _____ for it.

4. A _____ is a sign or object that shows where something is.

5. To _____ something is to want it very much.

6. Something _____ is very, very important.

7. When people are given jobs or things to do, they are _____ to them.

8. To _____ a ship or plane is to direct where it is going.

9. When you say or prove something is definitely true, you _____ it.

10. Conditions that are _____ are difficult and unpleasant.

◆ USE

Work with a partner and answer these questions. Use complete sentences.

1. What is something you might need to *confirm*?
2. What have you taken *credit* for recently?
3. What is something that you *long for*?
4. What do people take with them on an *expedition*?
5. How long could you stay outside in the *bitter* cold?
6. In what jobs do people have to make *crucial* decisions?

◆ EXTENSION: COMPOUND ADJECTIVES WITH NUMBERS

Look at the sentence from the reading:

> It was a **forty-mile** trip!

Forty-mile is a compound adjective. One way to form compound adjectives is to combine a number with a noun. In the compound adjective, the noun is singular even when the number is two or more.

(number) (noun)   (compound adjective)
a baby who is six months old = a <u>six-month-old</u> baby

Change the underlined phrases into phrases with compound adjectives.

Example: I work in a <u>building with twenty floors</u>.   *twenty-floor building*

1. He drives a <u>car with four doors</u>.   _____

2. She has a <u>daughter who is ten years old</u>.   _____

3. They went on a <u>vacation for one week</u>.   _____

4. I am reading a <u>book with two hundred pages</u>.   _____

5. She went to a <u>meeting for three hours</u>.   _____

6. It was a <u>flight that was ten hours</u>.   _____

Add three of your own compound adjectives with numbers. Use each word in a sentence.

COMPREHENSION

◆ UNDERSTANDING MAIN IDEAS

Circle the letter of the best answer.

1. Paragraph 1 is mainly about _____.
   a. the number of expeditions to the North Pole
   b. how Commander Peary took credit for reaching the North Pole
   c. the difficult conditions on the North Pole expeditions

2. Paragraph 5 is mostly about _____.
   a. how Henson played an important role on Peary's expeditions
   b. how Henson prepared for their North Pole expeditions
   c. why Peary and Henson made expeditions to the North Pole

3. The main topic of paragraph 9 is _____.
   a. how Peary treated Henson after they reached the North Pole
   b. how happy Peary and Henson were after they reached the North Pole
   c. how Peary was honored after his expedition to the North Pole

4. Paragraph 10 is mainly about _____.
   a. how President Taft helped get a job for Henson
   b. how Henson was treated after the expedition
   c. where Henson worked after the expedition

◆ REMEMBERING DETAILS

Circle the letter of the best answer.

1. Peary and Henson met _____.
   a. in a clothing store   b. on a ship   c. in South America

2. The first expedition Henson took with Peary was to _____.
   a. the North Pole   b. China   c. Nicaragua

3. Peary and Henson failed to reach the North Pole _____.

    a. three times   b. six times   c. seven times

4. When Peary and Henson were near the North Pole, they had to turn back because _____.

a. they didn't have the special equipment they needed	b. there were storms and freezing temperatures	c. Peary was injured due to frostbite

5. Peary assigned Henson to the first sled because _____.

a. he wanted Henson to arrive at the North Pole first	b. Henson was the best driver	c. Henson usually moved more slowly than the others

◆ ORDER OF EVENTS

Number the sentences 1–6 to show the correct order.

____ Peary and Henson made six expeditions to the Arctic.

____ President Taft helped Henson get a job in the U.S. Customs House.

____ Henson ran away to Baltimore to become a sailor.

____ Henson wrote *A Negro Explorer at the North Pole*.

____ Henson reached the North Pole.

____ Commander Peary invited Henson to join his expedition to Nicaragua.

◆ MAKING INFERENCES

The answers to these questions are not directly stated in the passage. Circle the letter of the best answer.

1. The passage concludes that _____.
   a. the six North Pole expeditions failed because the explorers didn't have experience or the right supplies
   b. the North Pole explorers showed skill, courage, and determination on their expeditions
   c. only Matthew Henson had the courage and skill to be a great explorer

2. The passage suggests that _____.
   a. Commander Peary always appreciated Henson's contributions
   b. Henson never wanted to be honored for reaching the North Pole
   c. Henson was not recognized for his achievements because he was African American

3. The passage implies that _____.
   a. Peary wanted to be the only person to get credit for reaching the North Pole
   b. Peary wanted Henson to arrive at the North Pole first and set up camp
   c. Peary didn't believe that Henson reached the North Pole first

DISCUSSION

Discuss the answers to these questions with your classmates.

1. Matthew Henson was treated unfairly, but he didn't say anything for 12 years. What would you do in the same situation?
2. Today many people go on adventure trips instead of relaxing vacations. Which would you prefer? Why?
3. If you could go anywhere in the world, where would you like to go? Why?

WRITING

On a separate piece of paper, write about an exciting trip you have taken or would like to take.

Example: *Two years ago, I went on a trip to Greece. The trip was so interesting and exciting for me.*

UNIT 10
NELLIE BLY
(1867–1922)

BEFORE YOU READ

Nellie Bly was a famous newspaper reporter. She was one of the first women to write exciting and shocking stories.

Discuss these questions with a partner.

1. What is the job of a news reporter?
2. What types of stories do people like to read in the newspaper or see on television?
3. Do you like getting news from the newspaper, television, or the Internet? Why?

Now read about Nellie Bly.

NELLIE BLY

[1] In the late 1800s, most American men expected women to stay home and be wives and mothers. So, most people agreed with the writer of a newspaper article titled, "What Girls Are Good For." The article criticized women who wanted to be part of a "man's world" of work instead of staying home. Nellie Bly strongly disagreed. As a matter of fact, she was so mad that she wrote a letter to the newspaper telling them exactly what she thought. That letter changed her life forever.

[2] Nellie Bly was born Elizabeth Cochran in 1867 in Cochran Mills, Pennsylvania, a mining town named after her father. She was one of ten children. After her father died, her mother remarried. Later she got divorced, which was very unusual in those days. Like other girls of her time, Elizabeth was educated at home when she was young. Later, she went away to boarding school for a year, and wanted to become a teacher. But her family had financial problems, so she had to return home.

[3] Elizabeth was 18 when she read "What Girls Are Good For" in the *Pittsburgh Dispatch.* She wrote an angry letter to the **editor,** George Madden. He was so impressed with her writing that he put an advertisement in the paper. He asked for the name and address of the person who wrote the letter. Elizabeth went to Madden's office and he asked her to write a story to respond to his article. She agreed and wrote an article in support of the working women of Pittsburgh. It appeared in the Sunday paper and people loved it. Madden immediately offered her a job.

[4] Respectable young women did not write for newspapers in those days. Female writers always used made-up names, called pen names. Elizabeth chose the name "Nellie Bly," which was from a popular song. Bly refused to write news about parties and other unimportant topics, like most female reporters. Instead she wrote about divorce, which was rarely discussed in public, and about the terrible working conditions in **local** factories. She wrote about the poor neighborhoods, and the problems of working women. Her stories were popular with the readers, but they were very **controversial.** Factory owners threatened to stop advertising in the paper if she continued to write them.

[5] Nellie Bly suggested a different idea to her editor. She wanted to travel to Mexico and write about that country and its people. Women never traveled alone in those days, so she took her mother with her. At first, Bly wrote beautiful descriptions of the country. But after a while she wrote about more important things, such as the differences between the lives of the rich and the poor. She also wrote about the **corrupt** Mexican government and the need for **reform.** Her stories were very powerful, but again, they were controversial. Eventually, the Mexican government forced her to leave the country.

[6] After she returned to Pittsburgh in 1887, Nellie Bly decided to move to New York. She wanted to write for the famous newsman Joseph Pulitzer. She went to his newspaper, the *New York World,* which was the most popular newspaper in New York City at the time. However, she wasn't allowed to meet Pulitzer. She was **desperate.** She pretended to be a reporter for a Pittsburgh newspaper who wanted to write a story about Pulitzer. She finally met with him, but instead of interviewing him, she asked him for a job. She suggested several ideas for stories and was hired

because of her idea to write about the terrible treatment of the mentally ill.

⑦ In order to write her story, Bly had to be admitted to the Blackwell's Island mental hospital to **investigate** the conditions there. She didn't know how to act like a mentally ill person, so she practiced in front of a mirror. She messed up her hair and dressed in old clothes. She spoke Spanish and burst into tears for no reason. She said she lost her money and didn't know who she was. Finally, the landlord of the boarding house where she lived called the police. Several doctors examined her and said she had serious mental problems. The doctors sent her to Blackwell's Island for ten days. Her reports about the living conditions and treatment were shocking. The hospital was dirty and the patients were treated very badly. The authorities investigated the hospital. Eventually, hospitals were forced to change the way they treated the mentally ill.

⑧ Nellie Bly's articles appeared on the front page of the *New York World* for the next two years. She was the most popular female news reporter of that time. She worked in factories and wrote about the terrible working conditions. She got herself arrested to see what it was like to be a woman in prison. Then she reported on how women were **mistreated** there. She wrote about the dishonesty in politics. She also wrote about some amusing things, such as when she took a job as a dancer in a nightclub. Bly always described her thoughts, feelings, and experiences very honestly, and people loved it.

⑨ Most people remember Nellie Bly for her famous trip around the world. The goal was for Nellie to go around the world in less time than the character in *Around the World in Eighty Days,* a popular novel by French writer Jules Verne. She left with one small suitcase and a money bag around her neck. First she sailed across the Atlantic Ocean. She then crossed the English Channel to France and took a train to the town of Amiens where she met Jules Verne. He was surprised at how young and feminine she was. From there she traveled by train, ship, donkey, wagon, and every other possible way across Europe and Asia. She survived a terrible storm while sailing from Hong Kong to Canton, China. Every day, the *World* published stories about her trip. They even had a contest to see who could guess the exact time when Bly would return. Everybody loved it. There were songs written about her and toys, clothes, and games named for her.

⑩ Along the way, Nellie Bly wrote all about her experiences in places that most Americans had never seen or even heard of. She made the journey in 72 days, 6 hours, 11 minutes, and 14 seconds. When she returned to the United States, she rode a special train from San Francisco to New York. Cheering crowds greeted her everywhere. In New York, there was a big parade for her. It was the **highlight** of her life and the best moment of her career.

⑪ Nellie Bly gave lectures for a year and then returned to writing. In 1895, she met a wealthy businessman named Robert Seaman on a train trip. Four days later they were married. He was 72 years old and she was almost 30. Bly left the newspaper. Seaman died nine years later and she took over his businesses and ran his factories. She always made sure that she paid the women the same as the men. She was successful for a while, but later lost all her money and went bankrupt. In 1914, Bly went to Austria to get away from her troubles. When World War I started, she couldn't get out of Austria.

⑫ In 1919, 54-year-old Nellie Bly returned to the United States. She had only a few friends and no family and very little money. One friend gave her a job at the *New York Evening Journal.* Two years later, she became ill and died. Unfortunately, some people thought that Nellie Bly was not respectable because of her trip around the world and her controversial news stories. So when she died, her body was buried in an anonymous grave without a marker. More than 50 years later, the New York Press Club dedicated a monument to her in New York City.

13 Nellie Bly is best remembered for her amazing trip around the world. Her editor called her the "best reporter in America." Not the best *female* reporter, but the best *reporter.* Most importantly, she was one of the first reporters to write about the problems of the poor working class and the many **injustices** in the world.

VOCABULARY

◆ MEANING

Match the words with their meanings.

___ 1. local	a. change made to improve something
___ 2. mistreated	b. in great need and losing all hope
___ 3. highlight	c. to ask questions about something and try to find the truth
___ 4. editor	d. treated very badly
___ 5. reform	e. person who decides what is printed in a magazine or newspaper
___ 6. desperate	f. the best and most important part of something
___ 7. corrupt	g. causing disagreements
___ 8. investigate	h. an unfair act
___ 9. controversial	i. dishonest
___10. injustice	j. near where one lives

◆ USE

Work with a partner and answer these questions. Use complete sentences.

1. What are some recent important *reforms*?
2. What are the names of some of your *local* businesses?
3. How do police *investigate* crimes?
4. What is a recent *controversial* topic in the news?
5. What is the *highlight* of your day?

◆ EXTENSION: The Prefixes *mis*- and *dis*-

Look at the sentences from the reading:

> Then she reported on how women were **mistreated** in prisons.

> She wrote about the **dishonesty** in politics.

The prefix *mis*- means "badly" or "incorrectly." The prefix *dis*- means "not" or "the opposite of." Both prefixes have negative meanings.

$$\begin{array}{cc} \text{(verb)} & \text{(verb)} \end{array}$$
mis- + treated = mistreated (treated badly)

$$\begin{array}{cc} \text{(noun)} & \text{(noun)} \end{array}$$
dis- + honesty = dishonesty (not honest)

Add the correct prefix *mis*– or *dis*– to these words. Then write down what each word means. If you need help, check your dictionary.

Example: *discontinue*   *to stop doing something*

1. _____spell   _____

2. _____please   _____

3. _____lead   _____

4. _____understand   _____

5. _____cover   _____

6. _____continue   _____

7. _____judge   _____

8. _____inform   _____

Add three of your own words with *mis*- or *dis*-. Use each word in a sentence.

COMPREHENSION

◆ UNDERSTANDING MAIN IDEAS

Circle the letter of the best answer.

1. Paragraph 3 is mainly about _____.
   a. Bly's reaction to the newspaper article that criticized women
   b. how women were treated by society in the late 1800s
   c. the events that led to Elizabeth's first newspaper job

2. The main topic of paragraph 7 is _____.
   a. what Bly had to do to write her story about the mental hospital
   b. the terrible conditions at Blackwell's Island
   c. the changes that were made because of Bly's story on conditions at the mental hospital

3. Paragraph 9 is mostly about _____.
    a. the reason for Bly's trip
    b. how people reacted to stories about Bly's trip
    c. what Nellie Bly did on her trip

4. The main topic of paragraph 11 is _____.
    a. Bly's marriage to Robert Seaman
    b. Bly's life after her trip around the world
    c. Bly's troubles and failure at business

◆ REMEMBERING DETAILS

Reread the passage and complete the sentences.

1. The article that made young Elizabeth angry was _____.

2. Bly traveled to _____ and wrote about the corrupt government.

3. Bly went to New York City because she wanted to write for

    _____, the famous newsman.

4. Some of the subjects of Bly's articles for the *World* were _____,

    _____, _____, and _____.

5. There was a big parade in New York for Bly when she _____.

6. In 1914, Bly went to Austria to _____.

◆ ORDER OF EVENTS

Number the sentences 1–6 to show the correct order.

___ Joseph Pulitzer hired Bly to write for the *New York World*.

___ Bly made her trip around the world.

___ Bly's businesses went bankrupt.

___ The Mexican government forced Bly to leave the country.

___ Bly wrote about conditions on Blackwell's Island.

___ Bly went to work for the *New York Evening Journal*.

The answers to these questions are not directly stated in the passage. Circle the letter of the best answer.

1. The passage implies that _____.
   a. in the late 1800s, many women had successful careers
   b. the idea of working women was unusual in the late 1800s
   c. all workers were treated well and fairly in the late 1800s

2. The passage concludes that _____.
   a. most people weren't interested in reading about problems in society
   b. Bly probably made many enemies during her career as a reporter
   c. the *New York World* newspaper didn't think Bly was an important writer

3. The passage suggests that _____.
   a. Bly's life was changed forever after her trip around the world
   b. Bly enjoyed fame and fortune throughout her entire life
   c. nobody appreciated Bly's writing abilities

DISCUSSION

Discuss the answers to these questions with your classmates.

1. Why are honest reporters important in a democratic society?
2. If you were a reporter, what would you write about?
3. What are some good and bad things about news reporting today?

WRITING

On a separate piece of paper, write about an interesting news story you read or saw on television recently.

Example:*An important news story on television was the death of John Kennedy, Jr., and his wife in an airplane crash. The story showed how unlucky the Kennedy family has been.*

UNIT 11
MARIA MONTESSORI
(1870–1952)

BEFORE YOU READ

Maria Montessori was the first female doctor in Italy and a famous educator. She created the Montessori method of teaching young children.

Discuss these questions with a partner.

1. What did you learn in the first years of school?
2. What kind of teachers did you have?
3. How does education today differ from education 100 years ago?

Now read about Maria Montessori.

MARIA MONTESSORI

[1] In 1882, 12-year-old Maria Montessori had a very serious illness. She turned to her mother and said, "Do not worry, Mother, I cannot die; I have too much to do." Even at a young age, Maria believed she had a purpose in life. She had already decided she wanted to be an engineer. Most women in nineteenth-century Italy wanted to be wives and mothers. But Maria was not an ordinary girl. She was highly intelligent and extremely determined. She never worked as an engineer. But she did become the first woman in Italy to become a doctor. Then she used her understanding of science and medicine to develop the Montessori method of teaching. By the time she was 40 years old, she was world famous.

[2] Maria Montessori was born in 1870 in the Ancona region of Italy. Her father was an engineer and builder. He was very traditional and believed that women should be wives and mothers. Her mother came from a well-educated wealthy family. She believed that women had the right to be educated like men. Clearly, Maria **took after** her mother.

[3] When Maria was 12, she told her parents she wanted to attend a technical school to prepare her for a career in engineering. She did very well in mathematics and science, which are important subjects for engineers. But her parents urged her to become a teacher instead because it was one of the few respectable careers for young women. Maria refused. "Never!" she said. "Anything but teaching!" Finally, Maria's father agreed to allow her to enter technical school. She was the only female student in the school.

[4] Maria completed her technical studies, and then shocked her parents once more. She told them she didn't want to be an engineer after all. She wanted to be a doctor. Her father was even more upset this time.

But Maria was determined to follow her dreams. She applied to the medical school at the University of Rome, but the director told her it was "unthinkable" for a woman to do such a thing. Maria then asked for help from the most powerful man in Rome, Pope Leo XIII. In 1893, Maria became the first female medical student in Italy. It was a very exciting, but difficult, time.

[5] The students in Maria's class **tormented** her with their mean remarks. Her classes were almost **unbearable.** In those days, it was completely unacceptable for men and women to see a naked body together, even though it was for school. So Maria was forced to study the human body by examining dead bodies alone at night. Her mother helped her study for her exams because the other students refused to study with her. Even her father wouldn't speak to her or help in any way. Everyone tried to make Maria miserable so she would drop out of school. Maria had a lot of **willpower** and she wouldn't give up.

[6] During her last year at school, Maria gave a lecture to the medical **faculty.** Many people came to hear her, but most came to laugh at her. Maria's speech was so amazing that the audience was **stunned.** Everybody applauded and **cheered**—even Maria's father, who didn't want to go to the lecture. Maria graduated in July 1896 and made history as the first female doctor in Italy.

[7] Maria Montessori practiced medicine in Rome for the next 10 years. However, she didn't make a lot of money because she often treated poor patients without charging them any money. She supported herself by lecturing at the University of Rome. In 1897, she worked in a psychiatric clinic. She wasn't paid for this work either. Montessori toured the city's mental hospitals and became interested in the treatment of **mentally**

retarded children. She was very disturbed by their living conditions. She went from one hospital to another and studied the children for hours. Eventually, she decided that the children could learn if they were just given the chance. She began to write articles and give lectures about her studies.

⑧ In 1901, Montessori became the director of a school for the education of mentally retarded children in Rome. Most people thought these children were hopeless. They were locked in rooms and treated like animals. The people who worked there threw food at them and kept them in rooms with nothing to touch or see or play with. Montessori believed that the children behaved like animals because they were treated that way. The first thing she did was to change their **environment** and their treatment. She gave them activities to do and things to play with. After a while, the children responded. They learned to read and write. They did things that no one believed they could ever do. Montessori's students did so well that they passed the national examinations given to other children their age. She was praised highly for her work. She was called a "miracle worker." Hundreds of newspaper and journal articles were written about her and her work with mentally retarded children. Montessori lectured about her findings and people everywhere wanted to learn her successful technique.

⑨ Maria Montessori's career was very **promising** at this time. She had fame and success, and she was excited about her future. She was also in love with her assistant, Dr. Guiseppi Montesano. When Maria discovered she was pregnant, she was forced to quit her job as director of the school. Unfortunately, Dr. Montesano didn't want to marry her. If anyone discovered that Maria had a baby and wasn't married, her career would be ruined. She went to the country to have her baby. Later she gave the baby to a family and visited him secretly. Nobody knew about her son until after her death.

⑩ Over the next several years, Montessori studied many subjects, including psychology and education, at the University of Rome. In 1907, she became director of the first Children's House school in a poor area of Rome called San Lorenzo. The school had over 50 students from three to six years of age in a single room. People believed that these wild children could not be educated or controlled. Again, Montessori gave the children work to do, things to play with, and the freedom to learn on their own. She allowed them to make mistakes and to learn from them. The results were amazing.

⑪ Soon her students could read, write, and count—even the four-year-olds! Visitors from around the world came to learn Montessori's teaching methods. She became famous everywhere. Within two years, all the kindergartens in Switzerland changed to the Montessori system. In 1909, she published a book called *The Montessori Method*. She continued her work by studying the needs of older children and developed teaching methods for them as well.

⑫ The success of the Children's House led to the opening of many other Montessori schools throughout the United States and Europe. The schools were for all children, not only those with learning problems. Alexander Graham Bell formed an American Montessori Society. Queen Victoria invited Montessori to London to honor the beginning of the use of the Montessori method in England. In Italy, Queen Mother Margherita supported the Roman Montessori Society. For nearly 50 years, Montessori lectured at training centers around the world. She wrote several books and never stopped working. She died in Holland at the age of 82. Her determination, independence, and hard work changed the world of education forever.

VOCABULARY

◆ MEANING

What is the best meaning of the underlined words? Circle the letter of the correct answer.

1. Montessori changed the children's <u>environment</u>.
   - a. subjects they liked to study
   - b. conditions in which they lived
   - c. things they were told to do

2. The students in Maria's class <u>tormented</u> her.
   - a. tried to be helpful
   - b. treated her badly
   - c. told her their problems

3. She toured places that cared for <u>mentally retarded</u> children.
   - a. having difficulty learning things that average people can learn
   - b. physically unable to do things that average people can do
   - c. poor, uneducated, and unwanted

4. Maria <u>took after</u> her mother.
   - a. got along with
   - b. acted like
   - c. lived with

5. Maria gave a lecture to the medical <u>faculty</u>.
   - a. doctors and nurses
   - b. students and parents
   - c. teachers in a particular school

6. Montessori's career was very <u>promising</u> at this time.
   - a. likely to be successful
   - b. acting like everybody else
   - c. changing very quickly

7. Her classes were almost <u>unbearable</u>.
   - a. very painful and unpleasant
   - b. difficult to understand
   - c. slightly unpleasant

8. Maria had a lot of <u>willpower</u>.
   - a. intelligence
   - b. physical health
   - c. mental strength

9. The audience was <u>stunned</u> by her speech.
   - a. disappointed
   - b. angry
   - c. surprised

10. They clapped and <u>cheered</u>.
   - a. laughed and smiled
   - b. shouted praise and approval
   - c. stood up and waved

◆ USE

Work with a partner and answer these questions. Use complete sentences.

1. When do people need to have strong *willpower*?
2. Who in your family do you *take after*?
3. What are some occasions when people *cheer*?
4. How do people act when they are *stunned*?
5. What *environment* do you prefer to study in?
6. How many teachers are on the *faculty* of your school?

◆ EXTENSION: THE PREFIXES *UN–* AND *IN–*

Look at the sentences from the reading:

> Her classes were almost **unbearable.**

> Her determination, **independence,** and hard work changed the world of education forever.

The prefixes *un–* and *in–* mean "not." Usually, we use these prefixes with adjectives, but sometimes we use them with nouns and verbs.

(adjective)   (adjective)
un– + bearable = unbearable (not bearable)

(noun)   (noun)
in– + dependence = independence (not being dependent)

Add the correct prefix *un-* or *in-* to these words. Then use each word in a sentence. If you need help, check your dictionary.

Example: *insecure I feel insecure when I speak in front of an audience.*

1. _____ formal   _____
2. _____ ability   _____
3. _____ grateful   _____
4. _____ believable   _____
5. _____ do   _____
6. _____ equal   _____
7. _____ accurate   _____
8. _____ beatable   _____

Add three of your own words with *un-* or *in-*. Use each word in a sentence.

COMPREHENSION

◆ UNDERSTANDING MAIN IDEAS

Circle the letter of the best answer.

1. Paragraph 1 is mainly about _____.
   a. Maria's sickness
   b. Maria's intelligence
   c. Maria's achievements

2. The main topic of paragraph 5 is _____.
   a. Maria's difficulties in medical school
   b. the behavior of the other medical students
   c. how Maria studied for her exams

3. The main topic of paragraph 8 is _____.
   a. the way the people that worked at the school behaved
   b. how Maria worked with mentally retarded children
   c. the accomplishments of the mentally retarded children

4. Paragraph 11 is mainly about _____.
   a. Maria Montessori's four-year-old students
   b. the use of the Montessori method in Switzerland
   c. the growth and development of the Montessori method

◆ REMEMBERING DETAILS

Reread the passage and answer the questions.

1. Why did Maria's parents want her to become a teacher?
2. How did Maria's father feel when she told him she wanted to be a doctor?
3. Who helped Maria study for her medical exams?
4. How did Montessori change the children's environment?
5. What subjects did Montessori study at the University of Rome?
6. Who formed the American Montessori Society?

◆ ORDER OF EVENTS

Number the sentences 1–6 to show the correct order.

____ Montessori asked Pope Leo XIII to help her.

____ Montessori started working with the poor children in San Lorenzo.

____ Montessori went to Rome's mental hospitals and studied the children.

____ The kindergartens in Switzerland changed to the Montessori method.

____ Montessori's students passed the national exams.

____ Visitors came to learn Montessori's teaching methods.

The answers to these questions are not directly stated in the passage. Circle the letter of the best answer.

1. The passage suggests that _____.
   a. by the late 1800s, most careers were open to women
   b. women did not have the same rights as men in the 1800s
   c. when Maria was young, many other women wanted careers in engineering and medicine

2. The passage implies that _____.
   a. the children at the school were not mentally retarded
   b. Montessori's early methods of teaching did not work well with mentally retarded children
   c. Montessori proved that mentally retarded children could learn if given the opportunity

3. The passage concludes that _____ .
   a. few people ever accepted the Montessori method of teaching
   b. Montessori's methods were only useful for teaching mentally retarded children
   c. the Montessori method was very different from traditional teaching

DISCUSSION

Discuss the answers to these questions with your classmates.

1. Do you think young children should have freedom in the classroom or follow strict rules? Explain.
2. In the United States, some mentally retarded adults live in "group homes." In a group home, a group of adults live together, away from their families, and are supervised by a health care worker. Do you think this is a good idea, or would most people be better off living with their families?
3. Some parents choose to teach their children at home, rather than send them to a traditional school. What do you think about this?

WRITING

On a separate piece of paper, write about a school experience or a teacher that you always remember.

Example: *When I was in junior high school, we had a math teacher. She was very smart, but she had a bad temper.*

UNIT 12

JACQUELINE COCHRAN

(1910–1980)

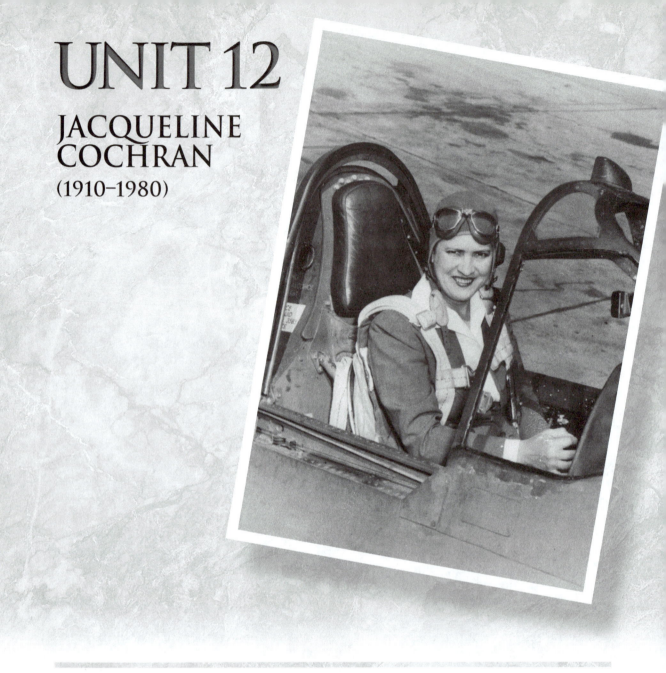

BEFORE YOU READ

Jacqueline Cochran was a famous airplane pilot who broke more flying records than any pilot in history. She was also a very important military pilot.

Discuss these questions with a partner.

1. What are some reasons that people join the military?
2. What is the position of women in the military today? Are women and men treated equally?
3. Would you like to fly a military plane? Why or why not?

Now read about Jacqueline Cochran.

JACQUELINE COCHRAN

[1] One day in May 1953, pilot Jacqueline Cochran was flying an F86 jet-powered fighter plane. Suddenly, she turned the nose of the plane down and dropped toward land at full speed. The plane went faster and faster every second. Then, the plane began to shake because the air built up ahead of the wings. Cochran was shocked to see that she was flying faster than the speed of sound. It was her moment of **triumph.** Then she **headed for** the airfield where many people waited to congratulate her. She was the first woman in history to fly an airplane faster than the speed of sound.

[2] Jacqueline Cochran **broke many records** in her lifetime. She was a very successful pilot and was famous all over the world. But she had very humble beginnings. She never knew exactly where or when she was born, except that it was probably in Florida in 1910. She was raised by another family in her town and never knew her real mother or father. Her family was so poor that they often didn't have enough to eat. Jacqueline's dresses were made from old flour **sacks,** and she didn't wear shoes until she was eight years old. She began to work when she was so young that she wasn't able to go to a regular school. A local school teacher taught her to read.

[3] When Jacqueline was just eight years old, she got her first job in a cotton mill. She was finally able to buy a pair of shoes! Two years later, she lost her job when the workers **went on strike** for three months. This seemed like a terrible thing at the time, but in the end it changed her life. Jacqueline found work at a beauty shop in Columbus, Georgia. Later, she worked at another beauty shop in Montgomery, Alabama. She worked very hard and became very successful in the beauty business.

[4] Cochran was always thinking of new ways to help her business. She decided that flying a plane would be good publicity for the beauty shop she worked in. So, in 1932, she began to take flying lessons. But Cochran was no ordinary student. From the first day, it was clear that she was a natural pilot. In three days, she had her first **solo** flight. In three weeks, she had her flying license! To get more experience, she worked without pay as a flight attendant. All she wanted was a chance to take over the controls and learn from the pilots. Jacqueline Cochran was soon ready to compete with men in the world of flying.

[5] Cochran was an excellent businesswoman too. In 1934, she started her own cosmetics business. But more than anything else, she wanted to fly. She also wanted to make money doing it. That same year she entered her first airplane race—the prestigious England-Australia air race. The prize money was over $10,000. Cochran and her partner flew a very fast plane. Unfortunately, the airplane had mechanical problems and they were forced to quit the race in Romania.

[6] Soon after, Cochran entered the Bendix Trophy Transcontinental Race in the United States. As she took off, her plane started to lose power. It was very foggy that morning and she couldn't see anything ahead of her. Somehow she got the plane off the ground, but she was flying so low that the antenna on her radio was torn off by a **fence** around the airfield. Once again, she had to leave the race.

[7] In 1938, Cochran finally succeeded in winning the Bendix Trophy. After she

received her award, she climbed right back into her plane and flew to New York. On the way she established a new cross-country speed record. Over the years, Jackie broke one record after another. At one time she held more than 200 national records. In her life, she held more flying records than any pilot in history, male or female.

⑧ In the 1940s, during World War II, Cochran realized that female pilots could help their country by flying planes to help in the war. She wanted to start a program for female fliers. But the U.S. government refused to believe that women could do the job. After two years, Cochran gave up. Instead, she went to England with a group of 25 female pilots and joined the Air Transport Auxiliary (ATA). They flew airplanes from the factories where they were built to the military units. This program was such a great success that the U.S. government decided to try Cochran's idea.

⑨ Cochran began to train American female pilots to fly military airplanes. The group was called the Women Air Force Service Pilots, or WASP. The training was very difficult because the women had to **master** skillful and dangerous flying. When they graduated, they tested both new planes and planes that had been repaired. They also flew planes that pulled **targets** behind them. Male fighter pilots used the targets for shooting practice. The WASPs learned to fly every type of military plane there was, from fighter planes to bombers.

⑩ The WASPs operated for two years, until the war was almost over. They received the same difficult training as male pilots and gave years of their lives to help in the war. But the U.S. government refused to give them official military **status.** Therefore, they didn't have the same rights and benefits as the rest of the military. They had no insurance. They had to pay their own way to travel to the training sites. They even had to use their own clothing at first. Thirty-eight female pilots died while they were part of the WASP program. But the government did not pay for their funerals or even the cost of bringing their bodies home. At the end of the war, these women who had trained, worked, and risked their lives for the war did not get any recognition or thanks from the military. Over 30 years later, President Jimmy Carter finally signed a bill that gave the WASPs military status.

⑪ After the war, Jacqueline Cochran went back to breaking records and winning flying medals, awards, and trophies all over the world. In 1954, she wrote a book about her life called *Stars at Noon.* Cochran met with presidents, kings, and other world leaders. She was named America's outstanding businesswoman and became president of the International Aeronautic Federation. She never stopped working, teaching, or learning. Jacqueline Cochran died in 1980. Her hard work and determination brought her a lifetime of excitement and success.

VOCABULARY

◆ MEANING

Write the correct words or expressions in the blanks.

break a record	sack	master	triumph	fence
head for	solo	status	target	go on strike

1. To do something _____ is to do it alone.

2. To go in the direction of something is to _____ it.

3. To learn how to do something very well is to _____ it.

4. A large bag made of a strong material is a _____.

5. A _____ is a complete victory or success, especially after a hard struggle.

6. To _____ means to stop working because of disagreements, usually about pay or working conditions.

7. An object, person, or place that is attacked or shot at is a _____.

8. A wood or metal wall around a piece of land is a _____.

9. To do something better or faster than anyone has ever done before is to _____.

10. Somebody's _____ is his or her official and legal position.

◆ USE

Work with a partner and answer these questions. Use complete sentences.

1. What are some things you put in a *sack*?
2. Why do workers *go on strike*?
3. What moment of *triumph* do you remember in your life?
4. Where do you *head for* after class?
5. What would you like to *master*?
6. What are some sports that athletes do *solo*?

◆ EXTENSION: WORDS ENDING IN *-o*

Look at the sentence from the reading:

> Somehow she got the plane off the ground, but she was flying so low that the antenna on her **radio** was torn off.

Generally, we form the plurals of words that end with a vowel plus *-o* by adding *-s*. Words that end in a consonant plus *-o* add *-es* to form the plural. There are some exceptions to these rules. One of the words in the exercise below is an exception.

(vowel + *-o*)
radio + *-s* = radios

(consonant + *-o*)
potato + *-es* = potatoes

Read the sentences. Each sentence is a clue for a word. Fill in the missing letters to complete each word. Then write the plural forms.

Example: *A small flying insect that bites and sucks blood*
     M O S Q U I T O   *mosquitoes*

1. A picture or word that is put on skin using a needle and ink
   T _ _ _ _ O   _____

2. A musical instrument
   P _ _ _ O   _____

3. A place an artist or photographer works
   S _ _ _ _ O   _____

4. A machine for playing CDs and cassettes
   S _ _ _ _ O   _____

5. The most important character in a play, story, or movie
   H _ _ O   _____

COMPREHENSION

◆ UNDERSTANDING MAIN IDEAS

Circle the letter of the best answer.

1. The main topic of paragraph 2 is _____.

   a. Cochran's world-famous flying records
   b. Cochran's poor and difficult childhood
   c. Cochran's lack of education

2. Paragraph 4 is mainly about _____.

   a. how long it took Cochran to get her flying license
   b. why Cochran worked as a flight attendant
   c. how Cochran became a pilot

3. The main topic of paragraph 8 is _____.

   a. why the United States didn't use female pilots during the war
   b. how England used female pilots during the war
   c. how Cochran used her flying skills to help during the war

4. Paragraph 10 is mainly about _____.

   a. what the WASP pilots did during the war years
   b. how the WASP pilots were not appreciated
   c. how President Carter finally gave WASPs military status

◆ REMEMBERING DETAILS

Circle *T* if the statement is true and *F* if it is false.

	True	False
1. Cochran's first job was in a beauty salon.	T	F
2. Cochran had to leave her first Bendix race because her plane's antenna was torn off.	T	F
3. At one time in her life, Cochran had over 250 flying records.	T	F
4. During World War II, Cochran went to England and flew aircraft for the military.	T	F
5. No American WASPs were killed during WWII.	T	F
6. After the war, Cochran stopped flying.	T	F

Number the sentences 1–6 to show the correct order.

___ Cochran served in the Air Transport Auxiliary.

___ Cochran started her own cosmetics business.

___ Cochran lost her job at a cotton mill.

___ Cochran started the WASP program in the United States.

___ Cochran worked as a flight attendant.

___ Cochran won the Bendix Trophy Race.

◆ MAKING INFERENCES

The answers to these questions are not directly stated in the passage. Circle the letter of the best answer.

1. The passage concludes that _____.
   a. Cochran's success was based on both courage and skill
   b. Cochran was a careful pilot who never took risks
   c. Cochran didn't enjoy flying; she just wanted to be successful and famous

2. The passage suggests that _____.
   a. many of the WASP fliers received awards for their bravery
   b. the WASPs were not accepted as equals by the military
   c. the WASPs could not fly as well as the other military pilots

3. The passage implies that _____.
   a. Cochran had a quiet life after World War II
   b. Cochran was a great pilot, but she wasn't as good as most male pilots
   c. Cochran's career helped make it easier for other women to become pilots

DISCUSSION

Discuss the answers to these questions with your classmates.

1. Do you like to fly? Why or why not?
2. Would you like to travel into space? Why or why not?
3. What do you think air travel will be like in the future?

WRITING

On a separate piece of paper, write about your favorite way to travel. Give your reasons.

Example: *My favorite way to travel is by airplane. It's fast, cheap, and comfortable.*

UNIT 13

ALTHEA GIBSON
(1927–)

BEFORE YOU READ

Althea Gibson was one of the world's greatest tennis players and the first African American woman to play world-class professional tennis and golf.

Discuss these questions with a partner.

1. Who are some famous female tennis stars?
2. Do you think a woman could win against a man in a tennis game? Why or why not?
3. Do you like tennis? Why or why not?

Now read about Althea Gibson.

ALTHEA GIBSON

[1] In 1957, Althea Gibson walked **gracefully** onto the tennis court in Wimbledon, England. She played like a champion. When the tournament was over, she had won the women's singles tennis title. A few months later, she went to the U.S. National Tennis Championship in Forest Hills, New York and won there too. In 1958, she won both tournaments again. During these two years, Althea Gibson was the greatest tennis player in the world. She was also an American hero.

[2] In those days, professional tennis was only open to whites. Gibson was the first African American woman to compete in these famous tournaments and the first African American person ever to win a tennis title. But her road to success was not an easy one. Althea Gibson was born in 1927 in South Carolina and was the oldest of five children. Her father worked on a cotton farm and her family was very poor. When the cotton farm didn't make money for several years **in a row,** the Gibson family decided to move to New York. They hoped that life would be easier there.

[3] Life was still difficult for Althea. She was often in trouble with her parents and teachers. She loved to **skip** school and go to the movies. She quit school at age 13 and decided to get a job. She worked in a mailroom and a restaurant, but none of these jobs worked out. She was fired over and over again because she skipped work just like she skipped school. By age 14, she was under the care of the New York City Welfare Department, which was a government agency that helped people in need. The future didn't look very bright for Althea.

[4] The social workers at the Welfare Department helped Althea find a **steady** job. They also urged her to join the local Police Athletic League sports program for young people. She played a few different sports, including paddleball, which was like tennis but played with wooden sticks called paddles. A musician named Buddy Walker often watched Althea play paddleball. She was very good, so he gave her an old tennis racket. Finally, Althea became interested in something other than getting into trouble.

[5] Walker saw that Althea had natural talent, so he arranged for her to play a few tennis games at the New York Cosmopolitan Club. The club members were so **impressed** by her that they paid for her to join the club and also paid for her tennis lessons. The following year, at age 15, she won the girls' singles title in the New York State Open Championship. In 1944 and 1945, she won the girls' singles title in the American Tennis Association (ATA), a league for African American players.

[6] When Althea was 18, she entered the ATA's women's singles tournament. She didn't win, but a **prominent** African American surgeon named Hubert Eaton noticed her. He knew she was very talented, so he offered to give her food, clothing, a place to live, and tennis lessons if she went back to school. Althea agreed and went to live with the Eaton family in North Carolina. The following year, she won the ATA women's championship. She went on to win this tournament for the next nine years in a row! Everybody was talking about Althea. Clearly, she was one of the best players in the game. Clearly, she should have been competing in major tennis tournaments around the world. But Althea wasn't invited to Forest Hills, Wimbledon, and other prestigious tournaments. That's because the clubs that held these tournaments did not

admit African Americans. Althea Gibson had had to overcome her poor background and her bad **attitude.** Now she had to struggle against racism.

⑦ In 1949, Althea graduated tenth in her high school class. Then she entered Florida A & M University where she studied physical education. During the next four years, she concentrated on her studies and continued to play tennis. She also did everything in her power to get invitations to various tennis tournaments. But they never came. Althea was **frustrated** and disappointed, but she was always dignified and professional both on and off the tennis court.

⑧ Finally, people began to support Althea Gibson. The editor of *American Lawn Tennis* magazine wrote an article against the "color barrier" in tennis. The article said that the race problems in the United States prevented many people from doing the things they wanted to do. Alice Marble, a popular tennis star at the time, said that people judged Gibson by her race and not by her skill. Finally in 1950, Gibson was invited to the U.S. National Tennis Championship at Forest Hills and the next year to Wimbledon. She became the first African American person ever to play in these tournaments. She didn't win, but she played like a champion and became famous.

⑨ In 1953, Gibson graduated from college. She thought about leaving tennis because she wasn't playing very well. She had dropped from seventh place to seventieth place in the national rankings, which was a list of all the female tennis players in the United States. Gibson moved to Jefferson City, Missouri and taught physical education at a college. Two years later, she started to play tennis again. In 1955, the U.S. State Department sent Gibson and three other American women to Southeast Asia and Mexico on a "good

will" tennis tour. Suddenly in 1957, Gibson started to play the best she had ever played. It was amazing. She won the singles titles at Wimbledon and Forest Hills. The following year, she won both of them again.

⑩ Althea Gibson's success was truly **astounding.** It was a great personal triumph and a great victory for African Americans. Gibson **eliminated** the color barrier in tennis by becoming the best player in the world.

⑪ In 1959, Gibson stunned the world when she retired from tennis. She was very honest about her reason. She needed to make more money. In those days, even the most successful male athletes made very little money compared to the salaries of today's professional players. For women, it was even worse. Gibson became a singer and actress, but she wasn't very successful. Then she did something else amazing. She began a career in professional golf. She competed in important golf tournaments. Again, she was the first African American woman to achieve this honor.

⑫ Gibson played in the Ladies Professional Golf Association (LPGA) tour from 1963 to 1967. During the 1970s and 1980s, she worked as a tennis coach. She wrote a book about her life titled *I Always Wanted to Be Somebody.* She established the Althea Gibson Foundation, which supports young people in poor city neighborhoods who want to play sports. She served on the New Jersey State Athletic Control Board and on the Governor's Council on Physical Fitness. Althea Gibson has made great contributions in many areas. She will always be a hero for athletes, women, and African Americans. As her book title said, she "always wanted to be somebody."

VOCABULARY

◆ MEANING

What is the best meaning of the underlined words? Circle the letter of the correct answer.

1. The social workers helped Althea find a <u>steady</u> job.
   a. permanent
   b. temporary
   c. well-paying and interesting

2. Althea was <u>frustrated</u>.
   a. very depressed
   b. violently angry
   c. annoyed and dissatisfied

3. She walked <u>gracefully</u> onto the tennis court.
   a. in an attractive, effortless way
   b. with long, heavy steps
   c. in a quick, nervous way

4. The club members were <u>impressed</u> by her.
   a. surprised and excited
   b. curious about
   c. full of admiration and respect

5. Gibson had to overcome her bad <u>attitude</u>.
   a. unusual past experience
   b. way of thinking and feeling
   c. activity that she was good at

6. She <u>eliminated</u> the color barrier in tennis.
   a. brought attention to
   b. removed
   c. improved

7. Althea loved to <u>skip</u> school.
   a. not go
   b. attend
   c. leave early

8. Gibson's success was truly <u>astounding</u>.
   a. understandable
   b. very surprising
   c. meant for someone else

9. A <u>prominent</u> African American surgeon noticed her.
   a. famous or important
   b. athletic
   c. friendly and intelligent

10. The cotton farm didn't make money for several years <u>in a row</u>.
    a. at the same time
    b. at different times
    c. one following the other

◆ USE

Work with a partner and answer these questions. Use complete sentences.

1. What are some things that people like to *skip*?
2. Why do most people like to have a *steady* job?
3. How do people act when they are *impressed* with something or someone?
4. How can you tell when a person is *frustrated*?
5. What was the last thing that *astounded* you?
6. Do you generally have a good *attitude* about things?

◆ EXTENSION: EXPRESSIONS WITH *In*

Look at the sentence from the reading:

When the cotton farm didn't make money for several years **in a row,** the Gibson family decided to move.

In a row is one of many fixed expressions that begin with *in.*

Replace the underlined words with one of the expressions using *in*, listed below. Use each expression once.

in a row	**in fact**	**in a hurry**
in charge of	**in case of**	**in private**

1. The new students stood <u>side by side in a line</u> in front of the class.   _____

2. Who is <u>responsible for</u> this department?   _____

3. You can call me at any time <u>if there is</u> an emergency.   _____

4. I must finish this <u>very quickly</u> if I want to catch the next train.   _____

5. Can we talk <u>without other people listening to us</u>?   _____

6. He looks like he is about 40 but <u>the truth is</u> he is over 50.   _____

Use each expression in a sentence.

COMPREHENSION

◆ UNDERSTANDING MAIN IDEAS

Circle the letter of the best answer.

1. The main topic of paragraph 1 is that _____.
   a. Althea Gibson was a graceful athlete
   b. Althea Gibson was a champion tennis player
   c. Wimbledon and Forest Hills are the world's most famous tennis tournaments

2. Paragraph 3 is mainly about the fact that Althea Gibson _____.
   a. couldn't keep a steady job
   b. had an unhappy future
   c. had behavior problems

3. The main topic of paragraph 6 is _____.
   a. the beginning of Althea's development as an athlete
   b. how the Eaton family helped Althea's career
   c. how people began to notice Althea's ability as a tennis player

4. Paragraph 12 is mainly about _____.
   a. the different careers Gibson had after she retired
   b. the financial problems of Gibson and other athletes in her time
   c. Gibson's success as a golfer

◆ REMEMBERING DETAILS

Reread the passage and answer the questions.

1. How did the social workers help Althea as a young girl?
2. Who was the first person to notice that Althea had talent as a tennis player?
3. Why wasn't Althea Gibson invited to the Forest Hills and Wimbledon tournaments?
4. Who helped Althea Gibson break the color barrier and get invited to the major tournaments?
5. Why did Althea Gibson retire from tennis in 1959?
6. How did Althea Gibson help young people in poor city areas?

◆ ORDER OF EVENTS

Number the sentences 1–6 to show the correct order.

____ Gibson qualified for the Ladies Professional Golf Association.

____ Gibson went on a "good will" tennis tour in Southeast Asia and Mexico.

____ Hubert Eaton offered to help Gibson and pay for tennis lessons.

____ The New York Cosmopolitan Club paid for Gibson to join.

____ The U.S. National Tennis Championship invited Gibson to play for the first time.

____ Gibson joined the Police Athletic League.

The answers to these questions are not directly stated in the passage. Circle the letter of the best answer.

1. The passage concludes that _____.
   a. very few people were willing to help Gibson achieve success
   b. Gibson's success came easily because she was a natural athlete
   c. Gibson had to work hard and overcome many obstacles to achieve success

2. The passage suggests that _____.
   a. Gibson was sometimes unsure about her abilities
   b. Gibson's bad attitude prevented her from making tennis her lifetime profession
   c. Gibson's battle against racism caused her to act badly during competitions

3. The passage implies that _____.
   a. professional sports in the United States has changed a lot since the 1950s
   b. by the 1950s, professional sports were open to anyone with skill and talent
   c. in the 1950s, racism was a problem only for African American women.

DISCUSSION

Discuss the answers to these questions with your classmates.

1. Why do you think the Gibsons thought life in New York would be easier than life in South Carolina?
2. The Eaton family helped Althea Gibson even though she was a total stranger. Would you ever do what they did? Why or why not?
3. How do you think tennis or other sports will change in the future?

WRITING

On a separate piece of paper, describe an experience you have had related to sports or the outdoors, such as winning a game or going on a camping trip.

Example: *Last summer, I went on a camping trip with two of my close friends. We stayed near a lake and there was nobody else near us.*

UNIT 14

GABRIEL GARCÍA MÁRQUEZ
(1928–)

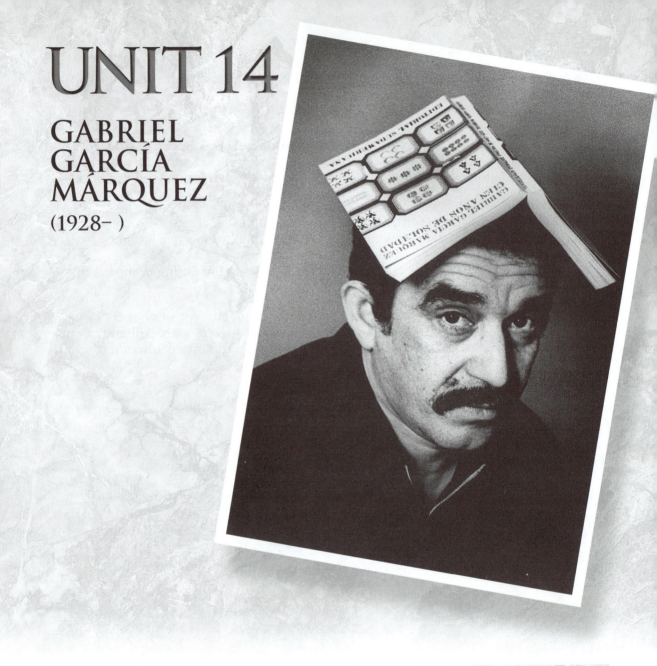

BEFORE YOU READ

Gabriel García Márquez is one of South America's most famous writers. Many of his books are about South American countries and their culture.

Discuss these questions with a partner.

1. What are some countries in South America?
2. What famous people do you know from South America?
3. What are some things about South America that you think Gabriel García Márquez wrote about?

Now read about Gabriel García Márquez.

GABRIEL GARCÍA MÁRQUEZ

1 Gabriel García Márquez was born in 1928 in Aracataca, Colombia. He was the oldest of sixteen children. His father was a telegraph operator who also wrote poetry, played the violin, and loved to read. Gabriel's parents were very poor because they couldn't find jobs in their town. They left the children with their grandparents while they went to other towns to look for work.

2 Gabriel became very close to his grandparents and his life with them had a great influence on his writing. Both of them loved to tell stories. Gabriel's grandfather was an officer in the army during the civil war in Colombia. He talked about the war and its heroes. Gabriel's grandmother and her many sisters also loved to tell stories, but their stories were very different. They liked to talk about ghosts, superstitions, and magic. When they told ghost stories, Gabriel got very frightened. He was so frightened that he was afraid to come out of his room after dark. His grandmother had a unique way of telling these unbelievable stories. She told them in a natural and **matter-of-fact** way so they seemed like the absolute truth. Márquez used this style later on when he wrote his greatest novel.

3 When Gabriel was eight years old, his grandfather died. He had to live with his parents again because his grandmother was going blind. There was no public education at the time, so he went away to boarding school. His parents were still quite poor and it was hard for them to pay for Gabriel's school. When he was 12, Gabriel applied for a scholarship to attend a private school in the capital city of Bogotá. He had to travel 700 miles by ship and train to take the scholarship exam. The trip took eight days. Three thousand students were competing for only 300 scholarships. Fortunately, Gabriel met a shy man on the train who **turned out** to be in charge of the scholarship program. He was so impressed with Gabriel that he gave him a scholarship.

4 Márquez completed high school in 1946, and people already thought he was a good writer. He went on to study law at the National University of Colombia in Bogotá. He became bored with his law classes and began to skip them and **neglect** his studies. Márquez walked around the city, rode streetcars, and read poetry instead of law books. He went to cafés and made friends with artists and writers. He began to read books by all the great writers of the day. He also began to write himself. He published his first short story in a Bogotá newspaper. During the next five years, 15 of his stories were published in Colombian newspapers and magazines.

5 In 1950, Márquez quit law school and joined the staff of a newspaper. He worked as a reporter during the day and worked on his own writing at night. He also continued to **associate** with other writers and artists. In 1952, his first novel, *Leafstorm,* was **rejected** by a publisher. He was very disappointed. He became **restless,** and in 1953, he quit the newspaper and found a job selling encyclopedias. The following year, he moved back to Bogotá and accepted a job with another newspaper.

6 Life changed for Márquez in 1955. The newspaper sent him to work in Europe. Soon after he left, the Colombian government shut down the paper. Márquez stayed in Europe but he had

nothing to do. While he was there, his friends sent *Leafstorm* to a different publisher. The publisher accepted it and Márquez was very happy. Unfortunately, the book didn't sell many **copies,** so he didn't make a lot of money. Meanwhile, Márquez went to Paris and had to **struggle** to survive. People helped him and he also made a little bit of money by collecting bottles on the streets. There he wrote two more novels, *No One Writes to the Colonel* and *In Evil Hour.* Eventually he left Paris and joined an old friend in Venezuela.

[7] In 1958, Márquez married his childhood sweetheart, Mercedes Barcha. He first asked her to marry him when he was 16 years old and she was 13. He thought she was the most interesting person he had ever met. She refused because she wanted to finish school. He waited for her, and 14 years later, they were married. Together they had two sons. Márquez continued to work as a reporter. He wrote stories about Latin America, including the Cuban Revolution in 1959. Márquez supported Cuban leader Fidel Castro and wasn't allowed to enter the United States because of his political ideas.

[8] For the next few years, Márquez didn't do much writing. He was depressed and thought he was a failure. His books did not sell very well. In fact, his most successful book at that time sold only 700 copies. Then one day in 1965, while Márquez and his family were taking a car trip, he suddenly got an idea for a book. He turned the car around immediately and headed home. He became obsessed with writing this book, and didn't do anything else. Mercedes had to sell the family car and almost every household **appliance** they had in order to support the family. Neighbors helped out by lending them money and anything else they needed. After eighteen months, Márquez finished writing. He was exhausted, but happy. In his hand were 1,300 pages of the greatest book of his career, *One Hundred Years of Solitude.*

[9] By this time he was so poor and in debt that he couldn't afford to mail the entire book to the publisher. Mercedes sold another one of their last small appliances and mailed half the book. By mistake, she sent the second half of the book first. A little later, she got more money and sent the other half. Fortunately, the publisher still accepted it. The novel was published in 1967 and immediately became a best seller. It has been translated into 30 languages and has sold more than 10 million copies worldwide. The story follows 100 years in the lives of the people of a small Colombian town. Readers love it because it talks about family, love, magic, politics, life, and death. Gabriel García Márquez was 39 years old and was suddenly very famous.

[10] Márquez received the Nobel Prize for Literature in 1982. Today, he lives in Mexico with his wife, where he writes, teaches, and participates in local politics. Márquez has written many books over the last few **decades.** All of them have sold many more than 700 copies.

VOCABULARY

◆ MEANING

What is the best meaning of the underlined words? Circle the letter of the correct answer.

1. Márquez went to Paris and had to <u>struggle</u> to survive.
   - a. do something that is difficult
   - b. be upset about something
   - c. get tired of something

2. The shy man <u>turned out</u> to be in charge of the program.
   - a. was part of
   - b. was in the past
   - c. finally proved

3. She sold every household <u>appliance</u> they had.
   - a. machine used inside the home, such as a stove or an iron
   - b. expensive furniture, such as a sofa or a table
   - c. tool for fixing a home, such as a saw or a hammer

4. She told her stories in a <u>matter-of-fact</u> way.
   - a. absolutely truthful
   - b. without showing emotion
   - c. with great emotion

5. Márquez has written many books over the last few <u>decades</u>.
   - a. 5 years
   - b. 10 years
   - c. 25 years

6. Márquez began to <u>neglect</u> his studies.
   - a. think about very hard
   - b. completely forget about
   - c. give too little attention to

7. His first book didn't sell many <u>copies</u>.
   - a. books that are exactly the same as others
   - b. books that are all different from each other
   - c. books that are very important or unusual

8. He became <u>restless</u>.
   - a. lazy
   - b. very angry
   - c. unable to relax

9. Márquez continued to <u>associate</u> with other writers and artists.
   - a. compete
   - b. spend time
   - c. appreciate

10. His first novel was <u>rejected</u> by a publisher.
    - a. not accepted
    - b. changed
    - c. praised for its greatness

◆ USE

Work with a partner and answer these questions. Use complete sentences.

1. What do *restless* people do?
2. What household *appliances* do you use the most?
3. Who are some of the people you *associate* with?
4. What things are easily discussed in a *matter-of-fact* way?
5. What do you sometimes *neglect*?

Look at the sentences from the reading:

In 1952, his first novel was **rejected** by a publisher.

Fortunately, the publisher still **accepted** it.

Rejected and *accepted* are antonyms, or opposites.

Choose the best antonym for the underlined words.

1. She makes the best pizza.
   a. worst   b. bad

2. Driving a motorcycle is dangerous.
   a. boring   b. safe

3. He neglected his studies.
   a. was upset about   b. cared about

4. She was nervous about the test.
   a. calm   b. happy

5. Some people criticized his ideas.
   a. agreed with   b. didn't understand

6. The paintings are priceless.
   a. unpopular   b. worthless

Use each of the correct answers in a sentence.

COMPREHENSION

◆ UNDERSTANDING MAIN IDEAS

Circle the letter of the best answer.

1. The main topic of paragraph 2 is _____.
   a. how Gabriel's grandfather fought in the civil war in Colombia
   b. how Gabriel was influenced by his grandparents' storytelling
   c. how Gabriel's grandmother frightened him with her stories

2. Paragraph 4 is mostly about _____.
   a. why Márquez decided not to study law
   b. how Márquez became a poor student
   c. how Márquez began to prepare to be a writer

3. Paragraph 6 is mainly about _____.

   a. Márquez's struggles as a writer in Europe

   b. how Márquez's friends helped him in Europe

   c. the publication of Márquez's first novel

4. Paragraph 8 is mostly about_____.

   a. how Márquez and his family lived while he wrote *One Hundred Years of Solitude*

   b. how Márquez got the idea for *One Hundred Years of Solitude*

   c. how long it took Márquez to write *One Hundred Years of Solitude*

◆ REMEMBERING DETAILS

Circle *T* if the statement is true and *F* if it is false.

	True	False
1. Gabriel's grandfather told him stories about ghosts.	T	F
2. Márquez prepared himself to be a writer by reading a lot of books.	T	F
3. Márquez went to Europe in 1955.	T	F
4. Márquez was not allowed to enter Cuba because he supported Fidel Castro.	T	F
5. The Márquez family had money problems while Márquez wrote *One Hundred Years of Solitude*.	T	F
6. *One Hundred Years of Solitude* made Márquez world famous.	T	F

◆ ORDER OF EVENTS

Number the sentences 1–6 to show the correct order.

____ Márquez wrote *In Evil Hour.*

____ Márquez quit law school.

____ Márquez received the Nobel Prize for Literature.

____ Márquez married Mercedes Barcha.

____ Márquez published his first short story.

____ Márquez found a job selling encyclopedias.

The answers to these questions are not directly stated in the passage. Circle the letter of the best answer.

1. The passage implies that during Márquez's youth in Colombia _____.
   a. many poor people didn't have the chance to go to school
   b. Márquez didn't think education was important
   c. the Colombian government wanted all of its citizens to be educated

2. The passage suggests that Márquez _____.
   a. became a writer because he wasn't smart enough to study law
   b. had a natural talent for and interest in storytelling
   c. was interested in writing because he wanted to make a lot of money

3. The passage concludes that Márquez _____.
   a. received a lot of support from his friends and family
   b. never depended on anyone to help him
   c. was famous because of his political contacts

DISCUSSION

Discuss the answers to these questions with your classmates.

1. Do you think art, such as painting and writing, should show political ideas? Do you like political art? Why or why not?
2. Many people today prefer to watch television or use a computer rather than read a book. Do you think that people may eventually stop reading books?
3. Márquez struggled to become a great writer. His life was sometimes difficult because he didn't have a steady job. If you had a choice between living like that, and having a more stable, predictable life, which would you choose? Why?

WRITING

On a separate piece of paper, write about a story that a family member has told you.

Example: *My grandmother told me a story about her sister Alice. One day when Alice was 13 years old, she found a bag with money in it.*

UNIT 15
DIAN FOSSEY
(1932–1985)

BEFORE YOU READ

Dian Fossey studied gorillas in Africa. She became famous for her fight to save animals that are in danger of disappearing.

Discuss these questions with a partner.

1. What are some of the endangered animals in the world today?
2. What are some things that are being done to help them?
3. Why is it important to try to save endangered animals?

Now read about Dian Fossey.

DIAN FOSSEY

1. Dian Fossey sat in the middle of a dense forest in Uganda, Africa. Near her, there was a group of gorillas she had studied for several years. A huge 450-pound male gorilla named Peanuts sat down near her. Fossey raised one of her arms and scratched herself with the hand of the other arm. Peanuts did the same thing. Then she held out her hand. Peanuts, who was six feet tall, stood up. Anything could happen at this moment. Peanuts looked like he was uncertain about what to do next. Then he reached out and touched Fossey gently with his huge black hand. Peanuts became very excited. He turned away and ran toward the other gorillas, **beating** his chest. Dian Fossey just sat there with tears of joy in her eyes.

2. Dian Fossey was born in 1932 in San Francisco, California. As a child, she loved animals and thought about becoming a veterinarian, which is an animal doctor. But while she was in college, she changed her mind. She decided to study occupational therapy, which is a way to help disabled people learn everyday skills. After she graduated, she moved to Kentucky and became the director of a children's hospital.

3. Several years later, she read about a doctor who had studied gorillas in Africa for a year and learned fascinating things about them. The more Fossey read about the gorillas, the more interested she became in them. In 1963, she decided that she wanted to go to Africa to see the gorillas. Her family and friends were surprised, but they supported her decision. She borrowed $8,000 from her bank and went on a seven-week trip to Africa. It was supposed to be a vacation. It ended up changing her whole life.

4. Fossey visited Tanzania where she met Mary and Louis Leakey, the famous British anthropologists. The Leakeys believed that by studying the gorillas they could learn more about humans. They needed people to study gorilla behavior to help their research. Fossey told the Leakeys about her interest in the mountain gorillas. They were very impressed with her. Even though Fossey fell and broke her ankle while visiting the Leakeys, she was determined to see the gorillas. Two weeks later, she went to the mountains and saw the gorillas. The experience was everything she had hoped for. She had to go back to the United States, but decided she would return to Africa.

5. One day while he was on a lecture tour, Dr. Leakey visited Fossey at the hospital where she worked. He wanted her to come back to Africa and work with him. By then, Fossey was 34 and she thought she was too old. She also had no training at all. But Leakey insisted that he wanted a **mature** person who was untrained and didn't already have opinions about things. All he wanted was someone with an open mind and a good pair of eyes.

6. At the end of 1966, Dian Fossey went to study with British scientist Jane Goodall at the chimpanzee reserve in Tanzania. She learned how to make observations and collect information. Several months later, Fossey set up her research station in the Virunga National Park in Congo. Immediately, she tried to get the gorillas to accept her. This was a very difficult task. At first they screamed and ran away when they saw her. But she was very patient. For months, she stayed near them in the forest and **imitated** their behavior. She walked on

her **knuckles** and chewed on wild plants. She beat her chest and made gorilla noises. Finally, they let her get close enough to sit and watch them and write her observations in a notebook.

7 Unfortunately, Fossey had other worries. The political situation in this area was very **unstable.** It was a dangerous place for a foreigner, especially a woman alone. Fossey didn't even have a two-way radio or any outside contact. But she didn't worry much about it and she was happy with her work. One day, the park director sent six guards to arrest her. They put her under "house arrest," which meant that she wasn't in prison, but she couldn't go anywhere. They did not allow her to continue her work with the gorillas. The park director said he did this to protect Fossey. But the real reason was that he was **suspicious** of her activities.

8 Fossey had to think of a way to get away. She told the guards that she had to go to Uganda to register her car. She left behind all her clothes and equipment. She brought only her notes about the gorillas. She got new supplies and set up the Karisoke Research Center in the mountains of Rwanda, just five miles from where she was before. For the next 13 years Fossey lived and worked with the mountain gorillas. She liked to be alone when she observed the gorillas. The Africans called her the "Lady Who Lives Alone in the Forest." Fossey had a new and unique view of gorillas in the wild. She discovered that they live in groups with a large adult male as their leader. They care for each other and will fight to protect an infant. In all the years Fossey studied gorillas, she found very few examples of **aggressive** behavior. In general, she found they were peaceful creatures and called them "gentle giants."

9 In the early 1970s, Dian Fossey went to the University of Cambridge in England to study for her Ph.D. in zoology. After she got her degree, she returned to Rwanda. With the help of some students, she **conducted** a count of the gorillas. It was clear that there were fewer and fewer gorillas. As the population of Rwanda grew, people needed the land for farming, so they cut down the forests where the gorillas lived. Also, illegal hunters, called poachers, hunted the gorillas for their skins and to sell them to zoos.

10 Fossey was devastated when some of her favorite gorillas were killed. She tried every way she knew to save them. By this point, Fossey's difficult life in the mountain forest was affecting her health. She was very weak. So she returned to the United States to rest and get her strength back. She raised money, wrote a book called *Gorillas in the Mist,* and worked on television programs about the gorillas. Many people around the world listened and wanted to help. Three years later, Fossey returned to Africa. By this time, Fossey had many enemies. The poachers, of course, hated her. The farmers who needed the land for growing crops and raising cattle did not understand her. The park directors who got money from the poachers were against her. Even the Rwandan government didn't like what she was doing.

11 On December 27, 1985, Fossey was found murdered in her cabin. During the night, someone had broken in and **stabbed** her. No one ever proved who killed her. Dian Fossey was buried at the Karisoke Research Station next to the graves of several gorillas who were killed in that area. On her grave are the words the "Lady Who Lives Alone in the Forest." Sadly, her **mission** to save the gorillas was never accomplished. They are still in great danger today.

VOCABULARY

◆ MEANING

Write the correct words in the blanks.

unstable	mature	mission	beat	stab
conduct	imitate	aggressive	knuckles	suspicious

1. To _____ is to do something exactly the same way as someone or something else.

2. When you hit something regularly or continuously, you _____ it.

3. The bones that connect the fingers to the hand are called _____.

4. Something you feel you must do because it is your duty is a _____.

5. Something _____ is easily changed or upset.

6. To be _____ is to be very forceful and ready to fight or attack.

7. To direct or lead an activity is to _____ it.

8. When you don't trust someone or something you are _____.

9. To push an object into someone or something using a lot of force is to _____ it.

10. A _____ person is older, experienced, and sensible.

◆ USE

Work with a partner and answer these questions. Use complete sentences.

1. What animals are *aggressive*?
2. How do people act when they have a *mission*?
3. How does a *mature* person behave?
4. What can happen when a government is *unstable*?
5. What kind of behavior might make someone *suspicious* of a person?
6. Do you ever *imitate* anybody? Explain.

◆ EXTENSION: PARTS OF THE BODY

Look at the sentence from the reading:

She walked on her **knuckles** and chewed on wild plants.

Knuckles are part of the hand. There are many words for different parts of the body, like "knuckle," that you may not know.

All these words are the names of parts of the body. Put each word under the correct heading that shows where it is on the body. If you need help, check your dictionary.

elbow	lash	gums	sole	temple
jaw	lobe	heel	wrist	pinkie
shin	palm	ankle	calf	scalp
thigh	thumb	shoulder		

HEAD	*ARM AND HAND*	*LEG AND FOOT*
_____	_____	_____
_____	_____	_____
_____	_____	_____
_____	_____	_____
_____	_____	_____
_____	_____	_____
_____	_____	_____

Add one more body part under each heading.

COMPREHENSION

◆ UNDERSTANDING MAIN IDEAS

Circle the letter of the best answer.

1. The main topic of paragraph 1 is _____.
   a. what Fossey did so the gorillas would accept her
   b. a surprising meeting Fossey had with a gorilla named Peanuts
   c. that Peanuts was a huge, but gentle, gorilla

2. Paragraph 5 is mainly about _____.
   a. Dr. Leakey's lecture tour in America
   b. why Fossey didn't think she was qualified to work with gorillas
   c. when and why Dr. Leakey chose Fossey to work with the gorillas

3. The main topic of paragraph 6 is _____.
   a. Fossey's research station in Virunga National Park
   b. that the gorillas were afraid of Fossey and behaved badly
   c. how Fossey learned to make observations and gather information on the gorillas

4. The main topic of paragraph 10 is that _____.
   a. Fossey worked hard to save the gorillas but many people were against her
   b. Fossey wrote a book called *Gorillas in the Mist*
   c. the Rwandans didn't understand why Fossey wanted to protect the gorillas

◆ REMEMBERING DETAILS

Reread the passage and complete the sentences.

1. As a child, Fossey wanted to be a _____.

2. Fossey didn't think she was qualified to observe gorillas because she was

   _____ and _____.

3. Fossey walked _____ and chewed _____. These
   were two ways that Fossey imitated gorilla behavior.

4. The real reason why Fossey was arrested was that the park director

   _____.

5. The Africans called Fossey _____.

6. When Fossey and her students counted the gorillas, they discovered that
   there were _____.

◆ ORDER OF EVENTS

Number the sentences 1–6 to show the correct order.

___ Students helped Fossey to count the gorillas.

___ Dr. Leakey asked Fossey to observe the gorillas.

___ Fossey met the Leakeys.

___ Fossey set up the Karisoke Research Center.

___ Fossey wrote *Gorillas in the Mist.*

___ Fossey saw the gorillas for the first time.

◆ MAKING INFERENCES

**The answers to these questions are not directly stated in the passage.
Circle the letter of the best answer.**

1. The passage concludes that _____.
   a. Fossey's work with the gorillas gave scientists new and important
      information
   b. scientists already knew much of the information Fossey gave them
   c. Fossey proved that gorillas are aggressive animals that can't relate to humans

2. The passage suggests that _____.
   a. Fossey was so dedicated to her work that she didn't think about her safety
   b. the Tanzanian government was very concerned about Fossey's safety
   c. Fossey was concerned about the political situation in Tanzania and feared for
      her life

3. The passage implies that _____.
   a. nobody has taken Fossey's place in the fight to save the gorillas
   b. other people now have to help to save the gorillas
   c. thanks to Fossey's work, the gorillas will always be protected

DISCUSSION

Discuss the answers to these questions with your classmates.

1. Do you think animals should be kept in zoos? Why or why not?
2. Two of the most famous scientists that worked with gorillas are women—Dian Fossey and Jane Goodall. Is there a reason why women might be better at this type of research than men?
3. Many medicines and beauty products are tested on animals before people are allowed to use them. Do you think this is right? Why or why not?

WRITING

On a separate piece of paper, write about your favorite animal and why you like it.

Example: *My favorite animal is the horse. Horses are beautiful and intelligent. They are also very useful animals for people.*

UNIT 16
BRUCE LEE
(1940–1973)

BEFORE YOU READ

Bruce Lee was a world-famous Chinese American martial arts expert. He was also a movie star and film producer.

Discuss these questions with a partner.

1. What are some forms of martial arts?
2. What fighting sports are there besides the martial arts?
3. How are the martial arts different from other types of fighting?

Now read about Bruce Lee.

BRUCE LEE

1 Bruce Lee was born in 1940 in San Francisco, California while his father, an opera singer from Hong Kong, was on tour there. According to the Chinese calendar, Lee was born during the Hour of the Dragon in the Year of the Dragon, so his family often called him "Little Dragon." But young Bruce was not like his nickname. He was actually a weak, sick child.

2 His parents gave him the English name "Bruce" for his American birth certificate. Bruce's Chinese name was Li Jun Fan, which is a girl's name. His parents were very superstitious and gave Bruce a girl's name to **trick** the evil spirits. One of their sons had died before Bruce was born, and they were afraid Bruce would die too. Bruce's mother even **pierced** one of his ears so the spirits would think he was a girl.

3 In 1941, the Lee family returned to Hong Kong. Bruce's father knew some important people that worked in the movie business. They helped Bruce Lee to become a child movie star. Bruce acted in his first movie when he was only six years old. By the time he was 18, he had appeared in 20 movies. In the movie *The Orphan,* Bruce played a **gang** member who was always in trouble. This was very much like his real life. Bruce didn't like to study and he got into trouble so often that he was thrown out of school. He spent most of his time in the streets fighting with other kids.

4 As a child, Bruce was small, thin, and weak and wore eyeglasses. Other boys **bullied** him, so he needed to protect himself. When he was about nine, he started taking lessons in an ancient Chinese way of fighting called kung fu. He practiced every day, and soon he thought about nothing else. Bruce became a better fighter, but knowing kung fu also got him into trouble. One day he was arrested after he was in a serious fight where some people were hurt. At that point, his parents decided to send him to America. They hoped he would stay out of trouble there.

5 When Bruce Lee arrived in the United States at age 18, his life changed completely. At first, he gave dance lessons in San Francisco's Chinatown. Then he moved to Seattle, Washington, where his father's friend owned a restaurant. Lee worked as a waiter in the evenings. During the day, he went to school and earned his high school diploma. Then he went to the University of Washington to study philosophy. After a while, he started teaching kung fu, and later opened his own school.

6 At first, Lee only taught other Asians. But eventually he opened his school to everyone. Some traditional Chinese people, or elders, were angry about this because traditionally the Chinese didn't teach their fighting secrets to non-Asians. They challenged Lee to fight with one of their kung fu experts. They were amazed when Lee won. The elders never troubled him again.

7 In 1964, Lee married one of his kung fu students, Linda Emery. They had two children, Brandon and Shannon. In 1964, Lee also won a prestigious international martial arts championship. A lot of people began to notice Lee. Everyone was amazed by his incredible speed and power. Lee developed a unique style of kung fu. He also concentrated on building up his body. Lee believed that meditation and concentration were just as important as exercise. He read every book he could find

on all types of hand-to-hand fighting. He ran, lifted weights, and did everything he could to improve his physical fitness. While he ate, he would hit his hand on the empty chair next to him to make it stronger. He did sit-ups while he watched television. He even kicked and punched in his sleep. He drank flower tea and different kinds of high-protein drinks. One way that he made high-protein drinks was to put steaks into a blender. In restaurants, Lee usually ordered two meals. His favorite meal was beef with oyster sauce. He also took huge amounts of herbs and vitamins. At parties he did push-ups using only one finger and he proudly took off his shirt when people asked to see his muscles.

8 In 1965, a television producer who saw Lee perform at the Long Beach Championships contacted him. He offered Lee the part of Kato, a crime fighter in the television series *The Green Hornet.* Lee was thrilled, and he accepted immediately. Unfortunately, *The Green Hornet* was only on television for six months. Lee was very popular, but it was hard for him to find other jobs. There were very few roles for Asians in Hollywood at that time. Lee was desperate because he needed to support his family. Finally, he decided to return to Hong Kong to make movies there.

9 In Hong Kong, Bruce Lee was already a star. *The Green Hornet* was on television there and his old movies were still in the theaters. A Hong Kong producer immediately offered Lee a starring role in a movie called *The Big Boss.* Then Lee made *Fists of Fury,* which was an incredible success everywhere in Asia. After that, he decided to make his own movie. He was the writer, star, and director of *The Way of the Dragon.* At that time, it was the most successful Asian movie in history.

10 Lee was both a superstar and a hero to his Asian audiences. Lee did all his own fight scenes, which was unusual. His movements were so fast that he had to slow down for the movies. If he moved at his normal speed, his arms and legs would be a **blur** on the screen. In his movies, Lee always played the average person fighting for people's rights. Sometimes he fought against foreign invaders; other times he defended a town against drug dealers. His movies always gave people hope and pride. The people in the audience often stood up and cheered at the end.

11 Soon after, a Hollywood studio offered to produce Lee's next movie, *Enter the Dragon.* It was a dream come true for Lee. Things were going very well for him, but life as a celebrity was very hard. Crowds of fans followed him wherever he went. He had a beautiful mansion in Hong Kong with an eight-foot stone wall around it so nobody could climb over. Every room was locked to prevent people from stealing. He worked very long hours and he missed his family. Lee started to talk about retiring soon, so he would be able to relax and spend more time with his family.

12 Only three weeks before *Enter the Dragon* was going to open in movie theaters, Lee died suddenly. He was only 32 years old. The cause of death was an unusual **swelling** of the brain. Lee was in perfect physical condition, so people were shocked by his sudden death. They began to spread **rumors** about him. Some people said Lee was still alive and would come back some day. Others said **envious** kung fu masters had killed him. Others said there was a **curse** on him. Sadly, this seemed to be true when Lee's only son also died young. At age 28, Brandon Lee was accidentally shot during the filming of a movie.

13 Kung fu was almost unknown outside of Asia before Lee amazed his audiences with his almost **supernatural** abilities. After his death, Bruce Lee became a legend. *Enter the Dragon* was a huge international success and martial arts became popular all over the world.

VOCABULARY

◆ MEANING

Match the words with their meanings.

___ 1. bully	a. place on the body that becomes bigger because of an injury or illness
___ 2. curse	b. to make a hole in or through something
___ 3. pierce	c. to make someone believe something that is not true
___ 4. gang	d. to scare or hurt small or weak people
___ 5. envious	e. something that people tell each other that may not be true
___ 6. blur	f. wanting to have what someone else has
___ 7. rumor	g. impossible to explain by natural causes
___ 8. swelling	h. wish that bad things happen to someone
___ 9. trick	i. something that is difficult to see clearly
___10. supernatural	j. group of young people who cause trouble and fight other groups

◆ USE

Work with a partner and answer these questions. Use complete sentences.

1. When was the last time you *tricked* someone or someone tricked you?
2. Why are *rumors* often untrue?
3. What are you *envious* of in other people?
4. Do you believe in *curses*?
5. Why do young people *bully* each other?

◆ EXTENSION: The Suffix -ous

Look at the sentence from the reading:

>Others said **envious** kung fu masters had killed him.

The suffix *-ous* means "full of" or "having the quality of." When you add *-ous* to some nouns, they become adjectives.

(noun)   (adjective)
envy + *-ous* = envious   (full of envy)

Make adjectives from the nouns in parentheses by adding *-ous*. Make changes in the spelling where necessary. If you need help, check your dictionary.

Example: *a poisonous (poison) chemical*

1. a _____ (fame) movie star

2. a _____ (danger) sport

3. an _____ (ambition) politician

4. a _____ (miracle) discovery

5. a _____ (nerve) parent

6. a _____ (mystery) disappearance

Use each adjective in a sentence.

COMPREHENSION

◆ UNDERSTANDING MAIN IDEAS

Circle the letter of the best answer.

1. Paragraph 4 is mainly about _____.
   a. what Lee looked like as a child
   b. how Lee got along with the other boys
   c. when and why Lee's parents sent him to America

2. The main topic of paragraph 7 is _____.
   a. how much Lee exercised
   b. Lee's habits and lifestyle
   c. how Lee behaved at parties

3. The main topic of paragraph 10 is _____.
   a. why Asian audiences loved Lee's movies
   b. how Lee did his own fight scenes
   c. what Asian audiences did in the movie theaters

4. Paragraph 12 is mainly about _____.
   a. why Lee died suddenly at a young age
   b. the strange similarities between Lee's death and his son's death
   c. the stories and questions surrounding Lee's death

Circle the letter of the best answer.

1. Lee was called "Little Dragon" because _____.
   - a. his mother wanted to trick the spirits
   - b. he was a weak and sick child
   - c. of the time and year he was born

2. As a teenager, Lee spent a lot of his time _____.
   - a. fighting in gangs
   - b. studying in school
   - c. traveling to the United States

3. The Chinese elders were angry with Lee because he _____.
   - a. didn't fight in the traditional Chinese way
   - b. taught kung fu to non-Asian people
   - c. beat their champion in a fight

4. When Lee filmed fight scenes for his movies, he _____.
   - a. hired a professional to do his fight scenes for him
   - b. often disappointed his audiences
   - c. slowed down his movements

5. After he became a star, Lee always _____.
   - a. attracted crowds of people
   - b. got into fights
   - c. got sick

6. People were shocked by Lee's death because he _____.
   - a. was young and healthy
   - b. had many enemies
   - c. had a curse on him

◆ ORDER OF EVENTS

Number the sentences 1–6 to show the correct order.

___ Lee wrote, starred in, and directed *The Way of the Dragon*.

___ Lee appeared in *The Orphan*.

___ Lee moved to the United States.

___ Lee opened his own kung fu school.

___ A producer offered Lee the role of Kato.

___ A Hollywood studio offered to produce *Enter the Dragon*.

The answers to these questions are not directly stated in the passage. Circle the letter of the best answer.

1. The passage implies that Lee _____.
   a. wasn't a good enough actor to be successful in Hollywood
   b. couldn't get roles in Hollywood because he was Asian
   c. preferred to make films in Asia rather than Hollywood

2. The passage suggests that _____.
   a. Lee's fame brought him wealth, but it also made his life difficult
   b. Lee was never happy working as an actor
   c. Lee was never a success outside of Asia

3. The passage concludes that _____.
   a. non-Asian countries aren't interested in martial arts
   b. Lee liked martial arts because he made a lot of money
   c. Lee was a major reason the martial arts became popular outside of Asia

DISCUSSION

Discuss the answers to these questions with your classmates.

1. Do you believe there was a curse on Bruce Lee?
2. Do you like action films? Why or why not? Why do you think action films are popular?
3. Many parents in the United States send their young children to kung fu classes. Do you think this is a good idea? Why or why not?

WRITING

On a separate piece of paper, write about a movie you have seen recently.

Example: *I saw the movie* Life Is Beautiful *last year and I will always remember it. It was about a Jewish family in Italy during World War II.*

UNIT 17

WILMA MANKILLER

(1945–)

BEFORE YOU READ

In 1985, Wilma Mankiller became the first woman to be chief of a major Native American tribe.

Discuss these questions with a partner.

1. What do you know about the history of Native Americans?
2. What do you know about Native Americans today?
3. Native Americans have some unique problems because of their complicated history. Are there any groups in your country with similar problems?

Now read about Wilma Mankiller.

113

WILMA MANKILLER

1 Wilma Mankiller was the first woman to become chief of a major Native American tribe—the Cherokee Nation. Many people didn't think a woman should have the position, but Mankiller showed them that they were wrong. She was an excellent leader and she brought progress, pride, and hope to the Cherokee people.

2 Wilma Mankiller was born in 1945 in Tahlequah, Oklahoma. Her father, Charlie Mankiller, was Cherokee. Her mother was Dutch-Irish. Wilma was the sixth of eleven children. The family lived in a small farmhouse without running water or electricity. The house was on a large piece of land called Mankiller Flats. Mankiller Flats was on a reservation, which is an area where the U.S. government let Native Americans live after the government took their land. In the 1800s, the government let Charlie's grandfather live there after the Cherokees were forced to move from their homeland in North Carolina to Oklahoma. Life was very hard in Oklahoma. The **soil** was not good for farming, so the Mankiller family had to struggle to survive. But they were a loving and happy family. Charlie Mankiller taught his children to love their Native American **heritage** and to be proud of it. He told them many stories about the history of the Cherokee people.

3 When Wilma was 12, the farm was destroyed after a terrible **drought.** The government offered to help the family move to a city. They believed it was better for Native Americans to leave the reservations and live among all different types of people. Wilma and her family didn't want to leave their home. But Charlie thought he could find work and give his family a better life, so they moved to San Francisco, California. They were very disappointed. The government had promised to give them money and jobs, but they didn't give them anything. The only job Charlie could find was in a rope factory. City life was very hard to get used to. Wilma missed her friends and the Native American community. Her classmates laughed at her name, her clothes, and her Oklahoma **accent.**

4 Wilma graduated from high school in 1963. She took some college classes and became a social worker. She loved her job because she liked to help people. She met and married an accountant from Ecuador named Hector Hugo Olaya de Bardi. They had two daughters and Wilma stayed home to take care of them. But she was unhappy. Wilma knew she wanted more from life. But she really didn't know what she wanted.

5 Around this time, many Native Americans were starting to **protest** against the government's treatment of their people. In 1969, a group of Native American students took over an empty prison on Alcatraz Island in San Francisco Bay. They wanted the government to give back their land and help the Native Americans improve their lives. Some of Mankiller's brothers and sisters went to Alcatraz and stayed on the island. Wilma couldn't go because she had young children, so she raised money to help the protesters. The students stayed on the island for 19 months. During that time, Mankiller decided that she wanted to dedicate her life to helping Native Americans. She took more college classes. Later, she set up a Native American youth center and created many programs for young Native Americans.

6 Mankiller's husband didn't like how she was changing. They disagreed about many things, so in 1974 they got divorced. Mankiller decided to return to Oklahoma **for good.** She went back to Mankiller Flats and built a house. She wanted to live among her people and learn about what they needed. She also wanted her daughters to experience a different way of life and to learn more about their Cherokee heritage.

7 Mankiller got a job helping the Cherokee Nation solve its economic problems. She went from village to village setting up programs and helping young people go to college. Meanwhile, Mankiller continued her studies and got her **B.A.** She loved her work and was very happy with her life. Unfortunately, her life almost ended in 1979. Mankiller was hit by a car as she was driving to class. It turned out that the person driving the car was her closest friend, who died in the accident. Mankiller was emotionally devastated and physically hurt. She had 17 operations and had to use a wheelchair for almost a year. Finally, she started to walk again. But soon after, she developed a rare disease that attacks the nerves and muscles. She had another operation and began to take a lot of medicine. Mankiller fought for her life again, and eventually she was healthy enough to return to work.

8 She started a project in an extremely poor community that didn't even have running water. She got government money to help make improvements in the town. They built new buildings and houses and put in 16 miles of pipe for running water. The project was so successful that Mankiller started the Cherokee Nation Community Development Department and became its first director.

9 In 1983, Ross Swimmer ran for the position of principal chief of the Cherokee Nation. He asked Wilma Mankiller to run as his deputy chief, which is like a vice president. Many people didn't want a woman to be in that position. But they won the election. Wilma Mankiller became the Cherokee Nation's first female deputy chief. Two years later, Swimmer became Assistant Secretary of the Interior for Indian Affairs. He had to move to Washington, D.C., so Mankiller took over as principal chief for the two years of Swimmer's **term** that were left. She was now the leader of more than 140,000 people and controlled a **budget** of $75 million. Mankiller was very honored. She worked hard and did an amazing job.

10 Wilma Mankiller won two more elections and served her people for ten years. During that time, she worked to create jobs, improve education, build businesses and health clinics, and create better living conditions in Cherokee communities. Mankiller always believed that the Cherokee people needed to work together and to solve their own problems. She helped them to help themselves. By doing this, she gave them pride and hope for a better future.

11 In 1995, Wilma Mankiller decided not to run for reelection and took a job teaching at a college in New Hampshire. She is an **inspiration** to women and Native Americans everywhere. Her hard work and dedication will continue to benefit the Cherokee Nation for many years to come.

VOCABULARY

◆ MEANING

Write the correct words or expressions in the blanks.

B.A.	inspiration	drought	for good	soil
term	budget	heritage	protest	accent

1. A _____ is a long period of dry weather when there is not enough water.

2. To _____ is to say or do something to show you disagree with something.

3. Students receive a Bachelor of Arts, or _____, when they complete their college studies in subjects such as history, literature, and language.

4. Someone or something that encourages you to do something good is an _____.

5. When something is _____, it is permanent and won't change.

6. A _____ is a specific amount of money and a plan of how to use that money.

7. A way of speaking that shows that someone is from a certain place is an _____.

8. The traditional beliefs, values, and customs that are passed down over many years within a family or nation are its _____.

9. The ground in which plants grow is the _____.

10. A _____ is a certain period of time that is limited and does not change.

◆ USE

Work with a partner and answer these questions. Use complete sentences.

1. What are some professions that require a *B.A*?
2. Why do people organize *protests*?
3. What are some things that are part of your country's *heritage*?
4. What are the causes and effects of a *drought*?
5. Why do people have *budgets*?
6. Who has been an *inspiration* to you?

◆ EXTENSION: ABBREVIATIONS

Look at the sentence from the reading:

> Meanwhile, Mankiller continued her studies and got her **B.A.**

B.A. is a common abbreviation. It is short for Bachelor of Arts. We use abbreviations in both written and spoken English. Some abbreviations use periods and some don't. Some abbreviations, such as USA, are spoken as individual letters. Others, such as NATO, are spoken as words.

> <u>B</u>achelor of <u>A</u>rts = B.A.

Fill in the blanks with the correct abbreviations. The full versions of the abbreviations are given after the questions.

UN²	M. A.⁶	PIN⁵
RSVP³	FBI¹	P. S.⁴

1. The _____ investigates crime in the United States.
2. The _____ is an international organization that helps to keep world peace.
3. When an invitation has _____ written on it, you must reply.
4. When you want to add a note after you have finished a letter, you write

   _____.

5. A _____ is a number that you use as identification when you use certain services, such as bank machines.
6. When you continue in college after you get a B.A., you study for an

   _____.

Personal Identification Number	*Postscript*
Répondez s'il vous plaît (Please Reply)	*United Nations*
Federal Bureau of Investigation	*Master of Arts*

Use a dictionary to find out what these abbreviations are short for. Use each abbreviation in a sentence.

a.m.	**p.m.**	**e.g.**
vs.	**etc.**	**B.C.**

COMPREHENSION

◆ UNDERSTANDING MAIN IDEAS

Circle the letter of the best answer.

1. Paragraph 2 is mostly about _____.
   a. the history of the Cherokee people
   b. the place the Mankillers lived
   c. Wilma's childhood and family heritage

2. The main topic of paragraph 3 is _____.
   a. how Charlie Mankiller forced his family to move to San Francisco
   b. how moving to San Francisco was difficult for the Mankiller family
   c. how the U.S. government broke its promise to help the family

3. Paragraph 7 is mainly about how _____.
   a. Mankiller finally found happiness and work that she loved
   b. Mankiller was nearly killed in a car accident
   c. Mankiller's determination helped her to work hard and get through difficult times

4. Paragraph 10 is mostly about _____.
   a. why Mankiller was elected for two terms as chief
   b. how Mankiller made the Cherokee people work together
   c. Mankiller's achievements as chief

◆ REMEMBERING DETAILS

Circle *T* if the statement is true and *F* if it is false.

	True	False
1. Charlie Mankiller was given a government job in San Francisco.	T	F
2. The protesters wanted the government to give Alcatraz Island to the Native Americans.	T	F
3. Mankiller moved back to Oklahoma to sell her land.	T	F
4. Mankiller's first job with the Cherokee Nation was as deputy chief.	T	F
5. Mankiller was driving to class when she was nearly killed in a car accident.	T	F
6. Many people didn't want Mankiller to be deputy chief because she was a woman.	T	F

◆ ORDER OF EVENTS

Number the sentences 1–6 to show the correct order.

____ Mankiller helped the Alcatraz Island protesters.

____ Mankiller married Hector Hugo Olaya de Bardi.

____ Mankiller took over as principal chief.

___ Mankiller got her B.A. degree.

___ Mankiller returned to Oklahoma.

___ Mankiller started the Cherokee Nation Community Development Department.

◆ MAKING INFERENCES

The answers to these questions are not directly stated in the passage. Circle the letter of the best answer.

1. The passage implies that Wilma's early childhood experiences _____.
   a. influenced her desire to help her people
   b. made her angry and bitter later in life
   c. had very little influence on what she did later in life

2. The passage suggests that Ross Swimmer probably chose Mankiller to be his deputy because she _____.
   a. had important government contacts
   b. was good at her job
   c. was a woman

3. The passage concludes that Mankiller taught the Cherokee people _____.
   a. to protest to get what they wanted
   b. never to change the way they lived
   c. not to rely only on others to help improve their lives

DISCUSSION

Discuss the answers to these questions with your classmates.

1. Are men better leaders in some fields and women better leaders in others? Why?
2. Why do some countries have women as leaders and others don't?
3. The Mankiller family had a hard time when they moved from Oklahoma to San Francisco. What are some problems that people have when they move from one place to another?

WRITING

On a separate piece of paper, write about a woman who has achieved a lot in life.

Example: *My aunt Julie has achieved a lot in her life. She went to the same school as my mother in a small town. When she was 18, she won a scholarship to go to Columbia University in New York.*

UNIT 18

RICHARD BRANSON
(1950–)

BEFORE YOU READ

Richard Branson is one of the wealthiest, most successful, and most adventurous businesspeople in the world.

Discuss these questions with a partner.

1. Who are some famous and wealthy businesspeople of the past and present?
2. What are some of the world's biggest companies?
3. Would you like to work for a big company? Why or why not?

Now read about Richard Branson.

RICHARD BRANSON

☐1 Richard Branson is one of the most successful business **tycoons** in the world. He owns over 150 companies and is worth over $3 billion. He is also a daredevil who loves all kinds of adventures.

☐2 Richard Branson was born in 1950 in the county of Surrey in England. He is the oldest of three children. Richard had a happy childhood. He was very close to his mother and she always encouraged him to do his best. But that was sometimes hard for Richard. He had very bad eyesight and also had a reading problem. This made school very difficult for him. He also hated school rules and regulations.

☐3 At age 17, Richard decided to start his own student newspaper. But it wasn't just an average school newspaper. It was for students everywhere and it had articles written by rock stars, celebrities, politicians, and businesspeople. With his friend's help and a small loan from his mother, he published the first **issue** in January 1968. The magazine was a big success. Two years later, Branson got the idea to offer his student readers inexpensive records by mail. He had so many orders that he decided to start another business. His mail order record company was called Virgin Mail. He decided to use the name *Virgin* because he had no experience in business.

☐4 In 1973, Branson wanted to help a friend record some music, so he started Virgin Records. It became the largest independent record company in England. Virgin Records recorded bands and singers such as the Rolling Stones, Phil Collins, and Janet Jackson. Branson couldn't stop there. By 1983, he owned 50 different companies. In 1984, he took a big **risk**. He started an international airline with one borrowed plane. The airline, Virgin Atlantic Airways, eventually grew into the world's third largest transatlantic airline.

☐5 In 1992, Branson sold his Virgin Music Group for almost $1 billion. By 1999, the Virgin empire was huge. Branson owned 150 companies with 24,000 employees. By then he had two airlines, a travel business, radio stations, hotels, recording studios, entertainment companies, restaurants, movie theaters, stores, and a publishing company, all with the Virgin name. He even bought an island in the Caribbean and spent $20 million on trees and plants, a beautiful ten-bedroom house, and two guest houses. Then he rented the island to some of the most famous people in the world, such as the late Princess Diana, director Steven Spielberg, actor Mel Gibson, and television producer and celebrity Oprah Winfrey. They paid $20,000 a night to stay there! The Virgin empire was worth about $3 billion and was the largest privately owned business in England.

☐6 People are amazed by Richard Branson. He has no formal training or schooling in business and does not know how to use a computer. He goes against all the established rules. Branson runs his business empire from his home in London. There is no central office or board of directors who make important decisions. All of his companies are different from each other and all are privately owned and operated, which is unusual. The one thing that all the companies have in common is that they all put their employees first and give them a pleasant place to work. Even when business is slow, Branson does not **lay off** employees. "It all comes down to people," says Branson. "There's nothing else that comes close....Everyone you hire is so important." He writes a letter once a month to all his employees to let them know what is happening in his companies. He also invites them to call or write to him with their problems and ideas.

7 A good example of how Branson works is the way he runs Virgin Airways. Most airlines today make money by cutting their costs and offering less service to their customers. But not Branson. Virgin Airways' first class section has video games and movies. There is ice cream and entertainment for children. There are full-size sleeper seats, a place to practice golf, and **lounges** with spa baths. There are also luxury services such as massages, manicures, and limousine service to and from the airport. Eventually, Branson plans to have private bedrooms in his planes.

8 Richard Branson is not afraid to do wild and bizarre things, especially if it means publicity for one of his new businesses. One day, a Virgin Airways flight attendant told Branson about her idea to start a wedding business. Branson encouraged her to do it and said he would help her. She soon became the head of Virgin Bride, a company that plans weddings and honeymoons. To publicize the new company, Branson wore a bridal gown. It was only one of the many **outrageous** things he does. He even arrived at his own wedding hanging from a helicopter.

9 Branson's adventurous **nature** has always led him to take risks in business. But that has never been enough excitement for him. He is as famous for his **death-defying** adventures as he is for his business achievements. He broke a record and became the fastest person to cross the Atlantic Ocean by boat. In 1987, he took a skydiving lesson and nearly killed himself when he accidentally unhooked his parachute. Fortunately an instructor rescued him in midair. Shortly after that, Branson traveled from the United States to Ireland in the largest hot-air balloon ever made. It was the first transatlantic crossing in a balloon. When Branson and his copilot reached Ireland, the winds were so bad that they almost died in the icy Atlantic waters.

10 In 1991, Branson became the first person to cross the Pacific Ocean by balloon. The trip from Japan to Canada was nearly 7,000 miles and the balloon went as fast as 240 miles an hour. There were many frightening moments, such as when the balloon lost two **fuel** tanks. They also went up too high at one point, which is very dangerous. They were supposed to land in Los Angeles, but they landed in the Canadian Rocky Mountains instead—nearly 2,000 miles away. Branson wanted to be the first person to fly around the world in a hot-air balloon. He tried four times between January 1997 and December 1998. On his last try it looked like he might make it, but a hurricane forced the balloon to land in the ocean off Hawaii.

11 Branson's dream of being the first person to travel around the world by balloon didn't come true for him; somebody else did it. It's hard to imagine what Branson will think of next, both as a businessman and a daredevil. When someone recently asked him about the future of his travel empire, he replied, "Virgin **Space**." Who knows? If anyone will fly people around space, it will certainly be Richard Branson.

VOCABULARY

◆ MEANING

What is the best meaning of the underlined words? Circle the letter of the correct answer.

1. He published the first <u>issue</u> of the student newspaper.
   a. picture
   b. assignment
   c. copy

2. Virgin Airways has <u>lounges</u> with spa baths.
   a. special seats for passengers with disabilities
   b. comfortable areas to sit in
   c. areas where meals are served

3. They lost two <u>fuel</u> tanks as they crossed the Pacific Ocean.
   a. material that is burned for making heat or power
   b. air used for breathing while flying
   c. liquid used for cooking

4. Branson is a business <u>tycoon</u>.
   a. owner of an airline or railroad
   b. someone who manages a large company
   c. businessperson with great wealth and power

5. Branson does many <u>outrageous</u> things.
   a. expensive
   b. shocking
   c. funny

6. In 1984, he took a big <u>risk</u>.
   a. something you do that everybody else wants to do too
   b. something that will definitely help you make a lot of money
   c. something you do even though it can be dangerous

7. When someone asked Branson about the future of his travel empire, he said "Virgin <u>Space</u>."
   a. the area far away from the Earth where the stars and planets are
   b. the area right next to the sun
   c. all the countries in the world

8. Branson has an adventurous <u>nature</u>.
   a. the way someone is
   b. life history
   c. way of doing business

9. Even when business is slow, Branson does not <u>lay off</u> his employees.
   a. pay a worker extra wages
   b. stop employing a worker
   c. get angry at a worker

10. He is famous for his <u>death-defying</u> adventures.
    a. very dangerous
    b. popular
    c. expensive

◆ USE

Work with a partner and answer these questions. Use complete sentences.

1. What are some things that people with adventurous *natures* do?
2. What do you find in a *lounge*?
3. Why do businesses *lay off* their employees?
4. What is the most *outrageous* thing you have ever done?
5. Who are some famous *daredevils* today?
6. Do you like to take *risks*?

◆ EXTENSION: Compound Adjectives with Present Participles

Look at the sentence from the reading:

> He is as famous for his **death-defying** adventures as he is for his business achievements.

Death-defying is a compound adjective. One way to form compound adjectives is to combine a noun or adjective with the present participle of the verb.

(noun) + (present participle) = (compound adjective)
death + defying = death-defying   (that defies death)

(adjective) + (present participle) = (compound adjective)
long + lasting = long-lasting   (that lasts for a long time)

Change each phrase into a phrase with a compound adjective.

Example: *A smell that lasts long*   *A long-lasting smell* _____

1. A car that moves fast   _____
2. A meal that waters your mouth   _____
3. A car that looks nice   _____
4. A process that consumes time   _____
5. An event that breaks a record   _____
6. An effect that reaches far   _____
7. A man who looks good   _____
8. A stove that burns wood   _____

Add three of your own compound adjectives with present participles. Use each word in a sentence.

COMPREHENSION

◆ UNDERSTANDING MAIN IDEAS

Circle the letter of the best answer.

1. Paragraph 3 is mainly about _____.
   a. Branson's first businesses
   b. why Branson's newspaper was successful
   c. how people helped Branson start his business

2. Paragraph 5 is mostly about _____.
   a. the businesses that make up the Virgin empire
   b. Branson's Caribbean island and the celebrities who go there
   c. why Branson sold the Virgin Music Group

3. The main topic of paragraph 6 is _____.
   a. Branson's education and training
   b. why people like to work for Branson
   c. how Branson runs his businesses

4. Paragraph 9 is mainly about _____.
   a. how Branson's personality affects his businesses
   b. Branson's daredevil adventures
   c. the fact that Branson likes adventure more than business

◆ REMEMBERING DETAILS

Circle *T* if the statement is true and *F* if it is false.

	True	False
1. Branson's student newspaper had articles by rock stars, celebrities, and politicians.	T	F
2. Branson started Virgin Records to help a friend.	T	F
3. Branson studied business in college.	T	F
4. To save money, Branson cut costs on Virgin Airways.	T	F
5. Branson broke a record when he became the fastest to fly across the Atlantic Ocean.	T	F

◆ ORDER OF EVENTS

Number the sentences 1–6 to show the correct order.

____ Branson started Virgin Records.

____ Branson tried to fly around the world in a hot-air balloon.

____ Branson started a mail order record company.

____ The first issue of Branson's student newspaper was published.

____ Branson was almost killed in a skydiving accident.

____ Branson owned 50 different companies.

The answers to these questions are not directly stated in the passage. Circle the letter of the best answer.

1. The passage implies that Branson _____.
   a. is mostly concerned with money
   b. isn't a very good businessman
   c. wants his employees to be happy

2. The passage concludes that _____.
   a. Branson wishes he had more formal business training
   b. Branson's wild behavior has made many people dislike him
   c. Branson's adventurous spirit has helped him to succeed

3. The passage suggests that Branson _____.
   a. does things his own way and doesn't worry about what others think
   b. is a lot like most businesspeople in character and personality
   c. believes in the traditional rules of business and tries to follow them

DISCUSSION

Discuss the answers to these questions with your classmates.

1. What kind of boss would you like to have?
2. Do you think businesses today are too uncaring, mechanized, and cold? Explain.
3. Richard Branson is very successful, even though he didn't go to college. How important is it to go to college today?

WRITING

On a separate piece of paper, write about an experience in which you were treated badly or well by an employee.

Example: *Last week, I went to my bank and the bank teller was very rude to me.*

UNIT 19
RIGOBERTA MENCHÚ
(1959–)

BEFORE YOU READ

Rigoberta Menchú is a Nobel Peace Prize winner who has spent her life fighting for the rights of the Indian people in Central America.

Discuss these questions with a partner.

1. What are some countries in Central America?
2. What famous people do you know from Central America?
3. What do you think Rigoberta Menchú did to help the Indians?

Now read about Rigoberta Menchú.

RIGOBERTA MENCHÚ

[1] Rigoberta Menchú was born in 1959 in the village of Chimel, Guatemala. She and her family were Quiché Indian. Like most of the **indigenous,** or native, people of Guatemala, they were very poor. Every year, her family spent four months living in their mountain village and eight months on farms working in the coffee and cotton fields. Rigoberta was just eight years old when she began to work.

[2] Life was terrible for the workers. Rigoberta's older brother died after a plane spread **pesticide** on the field where he worked. Rigoberta and her mother, Juana Túm, were devastated, but they had to continue working there. They worked for 15 hours a day picking coffee beans under the hot sun. Juana had to carry Rigoberta's baby brother on her back while she worked. The baby was hungry and sick, but the family had no money for food or medicine. Sadly, the baby died. Now another child was gone. They had no money to bury the baby, so a friend gave them a small box and some money. When the landowner found out that Rigoberta and her mother took time off from work for the burial, he was so mad that he fired them.

[3] They returned to their village, but things were bad there too. As Indians, they had very few rights and no say in the government. Everything in Guatemala was run by people of Spanish origin, even though the Indians were the **majority.** Most of the land was owned by a few wealthy families who took land from the poor people and treated them very badly. The Indian children went to work in the fields when they were as young as five years old. They never had the opportunity to go to school.

[4] As Rigoberta got older, she became stronger. By age ten, she could pick 40 pounds of coffee beans a day and cut heavy **branches** with a large knife. But she refused to accept this way of life for herself or her people. She always talked about how the Indians needed to improve their lives. She even talked about going to the capital, Guatemala City, someday to ask the people in the government to make changes. One day, when she was 14, she was picking cotton with her friend Maria. Suddenly they saw planes above them. The planes sprayed pesticides on the field and the workers. Maria got very sick and died, just like Rigoberta's brother. Rigoberta didn't understand how human beings could do this to others. She had to help her people.

[5] Rigoberta saw and experienced the injustices against the Indian people. She also learned about them from her father, Vicente Menchú. For 22 years, Vicente led a group of poor farmers who protested against the Guatemalan government. In the late 1970s, some landowners started to take farmland from the people of a small village. Vicente joined a group that was trying to stop them. Together they worked and fought to protect Indian-owned land and to improve the lives of the native people. Vicente became a hero among his people. But the landowners hated him, and they wanted to hurt him. One day Rigoberta and her family found him nearly dead by the roadside. Fortunately, local people hid him and helped him to recover.

[6] When she was in her late teens, Rigoberta went to work as a servant for a wealthy family in Guatemala City. She thought things would be different for her there, but she was wrong. She and the other servants were given little food, and

were treated badly. The children threw dirty dishes in their faces and shouted orders to them. Rigoberta would not accept such treatment. She left her job and dedicated her life to carrying on her father's work.

⑦ Rigoberta Menchú worked hard for her father's **movement,** the United Peasant Committee. She **distributed** information to the Indian people and helped to organize protests. But things only got worse for the poor farmers. One of Menchú's friends was killed after she refused to be the mistress of a landowner's son. The murderer was caught and punished. He spent just 15 days in jail. There was no justice for the poor people of Guatemala. Meanwhile, the government sent soldiers and police to kill anyone who was connected with the Indian rights movement. In 1978, the army killed 106 people, including many children, because they refused to move from their land. The Menchú family was in danger because of their political activities. Rigoberta often hid in convents, where the Catholic nuns taught her to read and write. She also learned to speak other languages. She traveled all the time so the police couldn't find her. While she traveled, she talked to the Indians about how they should fight for their rights.

⑧ In 1979, Menchú's 16-year-old brother and some poor farmers were **captured** and tortured by a group of soldiers. The soldiers watched and laughed as they burned the farmers alive. Still, the Menchú family continued to fight for justice. In January 1980, Vicente joined a large group of protesters who took over the Spanish Embassy in Guatemala City. The police started a fire to **drive out** the protesters. But the fire got out of control and Vicente and 38 others were killed. Soon after this, Juana Túm was kidnapped by the army, tortured, and left in a field to die. For several days she lay **in agony**. Finally, animals attacked and killed her.

⑨ Rigoberta Menchú continued her fight. In 1981, a group of soldiers almost captured her. She was in a church when they came to look for her. She bent over and hid her face with her long hair, and somehow the soldiers didn't see her. But she knew that the next time she might not be so lucky. So she moved to Mexico.

⑩ In 1983, Menchú wrote a book about her life called *I, Rigoberta Menchú: An Indian Woman in Guatemala*. The book was about her life and the 30-year fight between the Indians and the military government of Guatemala. Menchú wanted the world to know that over 150,000 Indians had been killed for no reason. Even in Mexico, Menchú never stopped working for her people. She gave speeches around the world and worked for the rights of all native peoples. She tried to return to Guatemala several times, but it was always too dangerous. Once when she went back she was arrested. The police let her go because so many countries protested her arrest and asked for her freedom.

⑪ In 1992, Rigoberta Menchú won the Nobel Peace Prize. She used the $1.2 million prize money to set up a **foundation** in her father's name to help native peoples. She said, "The only thing I wish for is freedom for Indians wherever they are."

VOCABULARY

◆ MEANING

Match the words with their meanings.

___ 1. capture	a. chemical substance that kills insects
___ 2. foundation	b. group of people who work together for a particular goal
___ 3. in agony	c. born in or belonging to a certain place
___ 4. pesticide	d. to take someone by force
___ 5. distribute	e. to make someone or something move away from where they are
___ 6. indigenous	f. in great pain
___ 7. branch	g. armlike part of a tree that grows out from the middle
___ 8. majority	h. organization that gives out money for special purposes
___ 9. movement	i. to give out or send something to different people
___10. drive out	j. most of the people or things in a certain group

◆ USE

Work with a partner and answer these questions. Use complete sentences.

1. What are some plants or animals that are *indigenous* to your country?
2. What nationality are the *majority* of students in your class?
3. Why do farmers use *pesticides*?
4. What are some popular *movements* today?
5. What do police officers do to *capture* criminals?

◆ EXTENSION: THE SUFFIXES *-MENT* AND *-TION*

Look at the sentences from the reading:

Rigoberta Menchú worked hard for her father's **move*ment***.

She used the $1.2 million prize money to set up a **founda*tion***.

When you add the suffix *-ment* or *-tion* to some verbs, they become nouns.

      (verb)   (noun)
    move + *-ment* = movement (a group of people who work together
                  for a particular goal)

      (verb)   (noun)
    found + *-tion* = foundation (an organization that gives out money
                  for special purposes)

Add the correct suffix *-ment* or *-tion* to these verbs. Make changes in the spelling where necessary. If you need help, check your dictionary.

Example: *educate*　　　*education*

1. produce　　　_____
2. enjoy　　　_____
3. employ　　　_____
4. satisfy　　　_____
5. govern　　　_____
6. excite　　　_____
7. improve　　　_____
8. pronounce　　　_____
9. arrange　　　_____
10. react　　　_____

Use each noun in a sentence.

COMPREHENSION

◆ UNDERSTANDING MAIN IDEAS

Circle the letter of the best answer.

1. The main topic of paragraph 2 is _____.
   a. that it was wrong for the landowners to fire Rigoberta and her mother
   b. planes spread pesticides on the fields and killed workers
   c. Rigoberta and her family suffered terribly at the farm

2. Paragraph 5 is mostly about _____.
   a. when and why Vicente Menchú became an Indian rights leader
   b. how the landowners took over the Indians' farmland
   c. what the landowners did to Vicente Menchú to punish him

3. The main topic of paragraph 7 is _____.
   a. the work Rigoberta Menchú did for the United Peasant Committee
   b. the pain, suffering, and death the government caused the Indians
   c. why Rigoberta Menchú was in danger and how she escaped

4. Paragraph 10 is mainly about the fact that _____.
   a. People protested when Menchú was arrested
   b. Menchú continued her fight for Indian rights after she escaped to Mexico
   c. Menchú tried several times to return to Guatemala but was stopped by the police

◆ REMEMBERING DETAILS

Reread the passage and answer the questions.

1. Why did a landowner fire Rigoberta and her mother?
2. Why did Rigoberta's friend Maria die?
3. Why did Rigoberta leave her job as a servant?
4. Where was Rigoberta Menchú hiding when the soldiers came to look for her?
5. What was the subject of Rigoberta Menchú's book?

◆ ORDER OF EVENTS

Number the sentences 1–6 to show the correct order.

___ Menchú worked as a servant.

___ Menchú's parents were killed.

___ Menchú won the Nobel Prize.

___ Menchú began to work for the United Peasant Committee.

___ Menchú ran away to Mexico.

___ Menchú worked in the fields picking coffee beans.

The answers to these questions are not directly stated in the passage. Circle the letter of the best answer.

1. The passage suggests that _____.
   a. the landowners tried to help the Indians improve their lives
   b. the people in power didn't want the peasants to be educated
   c. the government wanted the Indians to own some of the farmland

2. The passage implies that _____.
   a. the government sent the soldiers to protect the Indians
   b. the Guatemalan government thought the Indians' lives were not important
   c. the church and its leaders were against the Indian rights movement

3. The passage concludes that _____.
   a. the Indians fought with each other and couldn't work together
   b. the Guatemalan government didn't want to hurt the United Peasant Committee
   c. the Menchú family and many other Indians sacrificed their lives to get justice for their people

DISCUSSION

Discuss the answers to these questions with your classmates.

1. In many countries, children work at a very young age. What do you think about this? What can be done to make things better for children?
2. Pesticides are very dangerous, but many people believe we need them. What do you think about pesticides? What can be used to replace traditional pesticides?
3. Do you think the world is better or worse than it was 50 years ago in terms of human rights—the way people are treated? Explain.

WRITING

On a separate piece of paper, write about someone you admire and why. The person can be from the past or present and be well-known or not.

Example: *A person I admire a lot is the actor Paul Newman. He is an excellent actor and he also gives a lot of money and time to children who have problems.*

UNIT 20

DIANA GOLDEN

(1964–)

BEFORE YOU READ

Diana Golden is a champion skier and Olympic gold medal winner. She is also disabled.

Discuss these questions with a partner.

1. What are some sports that disabled people play?
2. What are some medical advances that help people with disabilities?
3. What laws exist today to help disabled people?

Now read about Diana Golden.

DIANA GOLDEN

[1] Diana Golden grew up a happy, but **awkward** child in Lincoln, Massachusetts. She wasn't very good at sports. In fact, she was always the last person to be picked to be on a team. Sometimes she wasn't picked at all. But there was one sport that Diana was very good at—skiing. Every weekend in the winter, Diana skied with her family. What she liked most was that she could do it by herself. She didn't have to wait to be chosen.

[2] One day when Diana was 12 years old, one of her legs **collapsed** under her. She thought it was strange, but she tried to forget about it. Later, it happened again. Her parents took her to a doctor. Unfortunately, Diana had bone cancer, and her leg had to be removed. After her surgery, Diana was very brave in front of her parents and doctors. But when they left her hospital room she cried for hours. She kept thinking about how miserable her life was going to be.

[3] Several days later, Diana asked one of her doctors if she could still ski. He said there was no reason why she couldn't. That made her feel much better. While she was at the hospital, Diana saw other children die from cancer. She began to realize that she was lucky to be alive.

[4] A few months later, Diana was ready to try skiing again. She was unsure of her abilities and she was afraid to fail. Her parents took her to a ski area that had a program called National Handicapped Sports. She saw other disabled athletes and she also met her ski instructor. He was a Vietnam war veteran with one leg, but he skied like a champion. He gave Diana the confidence and encouragement to make her dream come true.

[5] With hard work and determination, Diana started skiing again. It was amazing. Soon she was skiing as well as she had before. One day during her junior year of high school, the school skiing coach saw her practicing. He asked her to work out with the ski team. She started to train to make her body stronger, especially her leg, back, and arms. A year later, she competed in the World Games for Disabled Athletes in Norway. That same year, she won the downhill event in the World Handicapped Championships. Diana was filled with **enthusiasm.** She thought of nothing else but skiing, racing, and winning. Eventually Diana became the star of the United States Disabled Ski Team. Newspapers and magazines published articles about her. They called her a champion and a hero. But Diana didn't believe she was a hero. She was just doing her best.

[6] After high school, Diana went to Dartmouth College. She trained with the ski team there in the school **stadium.** She had to use crutches to help her, but she ran and **hopped** up the stadium steps. There was a baseball field near the stadium where Diana worked out. Another student named Steve Brosnihan noticed her while he practiced. He admired her and liked her from a distance. But she didn't notice him.

[7] During her second year at Dartmouth, Diana quit skiing. She felt confused about her future. She didn't know who she was or what she wanted to do with her life. She began to search for meaning in her life. She joined a religious group. She studied and read. But after a while, she realized how much she missed skiing.

[8] After she graduated in 1984, Diana returned to skiing. She worked harder than

ever to build up her strength again. She trained with both disabled and non-disabled skiers. With great determination, she began to build the greatest career in the history of disabled sports. In all, Diana Golden won 29 gold medals in world and national championships, including an Olympic gold medal in 1988. Throughout the 1980s, she continued to win medals and awards in both disabled and regular events. In 1988, she was named U.S. Alpine Skier of the Year. The U.S. Olympic Committee named her Female Skier of the Year. In 1991, she received the prestigious Flo Hyman Award presented by the Women's Sports Foundation.

⑨ Diana was **on top of the world.** She had a wonderful personality, a bright smile, and high spirits. She was smart and funny. Over the years, she did a lot for the disabled athletes movement. Because of her efforts and triumphs, people began to see disabled athletes as true athletes first, not just as disabled people. Diana was an inspiration to many people. She shared her feelings and experiences in articles, television talk shows, and speeches she gave around the country. She told people that they can have their dreams and overcome any problems.

⑩ In 1991, at age 27, Golden retired from competitive skiing. She continued other challenges. She liked to go **hiking** and rock climbing in the hot desert. Her life was calm for a while, but she soon got terrible news. In 1992, the doctors told her she had breast cancer. She had to have both breasts removed. She was brave in front of others, just like when she was a child. But inside she was afraid and angry. Several months later, there was more bad news. Her cancer had spread and she needed more surgery and more treatments. Golden became very depressed. One night, she took an overdose of pills. But she realized she had made a mistake and she called a friend. Her friend rushed her to the hospital, and thankfully, she survived.

⑪ After her suicide attempt, Golden searched for reasons to live. She got a **puppy** but a month later it died. One day, she got in her car and headed for the mountains. She was going to jump into a deep river. But once again, her will to live was too strong. She turned back and went to see a **counselor.** She got another puppy and named him "Midnight Sun" because he was her "light in the night."

⑫ Golden tried to make the best of things, even though it was sometimes difficult. She had a lot of friends, and she liked to go out and have fun. One night she met a man at a Halloween costume party. He was Steve Brosnihan, the student who had watched her train at Dartmouth. It seemed as if **fate** had brought them together again. On Valentine's Day while Diana was at the hospital getting her cancer treatment, Steve asked her to marry him. By then, the doctors had told Diana that she had one to five years to live. Steve and Diana got married in August 1999 and said in front of everyone there that they would love each other forever. They have learned to make the best of every moment they have together.

VOCABULARY

◆ MEANING

Match the words with their meanings.

___ 1. on top of the world	a. young dog
___ 2. stadium	b. to jump on one leg or with two feet close together
___ 3. fate	c. to take a long walk in the country or in the mountains
___ 4. hike	d. someone whose job is to help people with personal problems
___ 5. awkward	e. large outdoor sports field that has many rows of seats
___ 6. puppy	f. strong feeling of interest in something
___ 7. enthusiasm	g. power which some people believe controls what happens in people's lives
___ 8. hop	h. not able to move the body easily or skillfully
___ 9. counselor	i. to fall down suddenly
___10. collapse	j. very happy

◆ USE

Work with a partner and answer these questions. Use complete sentences.

1. What is the name of the *stadium* that is nearest to your home?
2. How do people show their *enthusiasm*?
3. When was the last time you were *on top of the world*?
4. What are some things a *puppy* needs to learn?
5. What are some animals that *hop*?
6. Where do you like to go *hiking*?

◆ EXTENSION: EXPRESSIONS WITH *GO*

Look at the sentence from the reading:

She liked to **go hiking**.

Go hiking is one of many fixed expressions that use *go* plus the gerund (*-ing* form). These expressions are generally used to express recreational activities.

Add the word *go* where appropriate.

1._____ shopping   6._____ dancing

2._____ singing   7._____ eating

3._____ swimming   8._____ running

4._____ sleeping   9._____ laughing

5._____ jumping   10._____ camping

Add three of your own expressions with *go* plus a gerund. Use each expression in a sentence.

COMPREHENSION

◆ UNDERSTANDING MAIN IDEAS

Circle the letter of the best answer.

1. Paragraph 1 is mainly about _____.
   a. Diana's family life when she was a child
   b. how Diana started skiing and why she liked it
   c. how other children in team sports treated Diana

2. The main topic of paragraph 5 is that _____.
   a. Diana trained to strengthen her body
   b. Diana developed into a champion skier
   c. Diana won many awards

3. Paragraph 8 is mostly about _____.
   a. Diana's achievements as a skier
   b. how Diana started to train again
   c. why Diana decided to return to skiing

4. The main topic of paragraph 10 is _____.
   a. Diana's retirement from competitive skiing
   b. how Diana dealt with all her challenges
   c. how Diana's cancer was treated

◆ REMEMBERING DETAILS

Reread the passage and complete the sentences.

1. As a child, Diana liked skiing because _____.

2. Diana started to train to make her _____, _____, and _____ stronger.

3. Eventually Diana became a star. Newspapers and magazines called her

   _____.

4. After Golden retired from skiing, she enjoyed other outdoor activities such

   as _____ and _____.

5. Golden named her puppy _____ because he brought light and happiness to her life.

6. Steve proposed to Golden on _____.

◆ ORDER OF EVENTS

Number the sentences 1–6 to show the correct order.

___ Golden attended Dartmouth College.

___ Golden quit skiing temporarily.

___ A high school skiing coach asked Golden to train with the ski team.

___ Golden attended a program of National Handicapped Sports.

___ Golden won the downhill at the World Handicapped Championships.

___ Golden won an Olympic gold medal.

◆ MAKING INFERENCES

The answers to these questions are not directly stated in the passage. Circle the letter of the best answer.

1. The passage implies that after Diana lost her leg, _____.
   a. it took a lot of courage and determination for her to try skiing again
   b. Diana knew right away that she would ski again
   c. it was difficult for her to learn to ski again because she was so depressed

2. The passage concludes that _____.
   a. Diana helped to change people's attitudes about disabled athletes
   b. Diana was the first professional disabled athlete
   c. Diana believed that disabled and nondisabled athletes should never compete against each other

3. The passage implies that _____.
   a. Golden helped herself but didn't help others
   b. Golden was an inspiration to many different people—not just disabled athletes
   c. Golden was afraid to talk about her feelings about being disabled

DISCUSSION

Discuss the answers to these questions with your classmates.

1. Why do you think the World Games for Disabled Athletes are important for people with disabilities? Why are they important for people without disabilities?

2. In some ways, life today is easier for people with disabilities, and in other ways it is harder. For example, there are many types of new equipment and medicine that can help people, but they are very expensive. What are some other ways that modern life is both easier and harder for people with disabilities?

3. When Steve and Diana met at the Halloween party, it seemed like it was fate—that it was always meant to be, even though they hadn't seen each other in years. Do you believe in fate? Have you or someone you know ever had an experience like this?

WRITING

On a separate piece of paper, describe the qualities you think are important in a husband, wife, or life partner.

Example: *I would like to marry a man who is kind and understanding. I would also like him to know what he wants out of life and to work hard for it.*

ANSWER KEY

Answers not given will vary.

Unit 1   Leonardo da Vinci
Meaning: **1.** b   **2.** a   **3.** c   **4.** b
5. a   **6.** c   **7.** c   **8.** a   **9.** b   **10.** c
Extension: **1.** make   **2.** make
3. do   **4.** make   **5.** do   **6.** make
7. do   **8.** do   **9.** make   **10.** make
Understanding Main Ideas: **1.** b
2. b   **3.** c   **4.** b
Remembering Details: **1.** F   **2.** F
3. T   **4.** T   **5.** F   **6.** T
Order of Events: 3, 1, 2, 6, 5, 4
Making Inferences: **1.** c   **2.** a   **3.** b

Unit 2   Peter the Great
Meaning: **1.** g   **2.** h   **3.** f   **4.** b
5. a   **6.** e   **7.** c   **8.** d   **9.** j   **10.** i
Extension: **1.** harmless   **3.** timeless
4. useless   **5.** friendless   **6.** tasteless
8. homeless   **9.** colorless
10. sleepless   **11.** meaningless
Understanding Main Ideas: **1.** c
2. c   **3.** b   **4.** a
Remembering Details: **1.** He
wanted to learn everything about
European culture, science, and
education.   **2.** He wanted to be free
to study and learn.   **3.** They said they
were peculiar and had bad manners.
4. The Bishop of Salisbury taught
Peter about religion and government.
5. They wore European clothes; they
no longer painted their teeth and
they could choose their own
husbands.   **6.** It took 10 years.
Order of Events: 4, 1, 6, 3, 5, 2
Making Inferences: **1.** b   **2.** b   **3.** a

Unit 3   Ludwig van
Beethoven
Meaning: **1.** incredible   **2.** applaud
3. landlord   **4.** patience   **5.** torture
6. bad-tempered   **7.** insulting
8. independent   **9.** selfish
10. rebellious
Extension: **1.** an open-minded
person   **2.** a coffee-colored hat
3. a kind-hearted woman   **4.** a two-
wheeled bicycle   **5.** a blond-haired
actor   **6.** high-priced clothes
Understanding Main Ideas: **1.** a

2. a   **3.** b   **4.** a
Remembering Details: **1.** b   **2.** b
3. a   **4.** c   **5.** b   **6.** b
Order of Events: 3, 6, 1, 5, 4, 2
Making Inferences: **1.** c   **2.** c   **3.** b

Unit 4   Fyodor Dostoyevsky
Meaning: **1.** c   **2.** b   **3.** a   **4.** c
5. b   **6.** c   **7.** b   **8.** b   **9.** c   **10.** a
Extension: First part: equality,
illness, seriousness, similarity,
weakness, neatness, popularity,
darkness   Second part: **1.** darkness
2. neatness   **3.** weakness
4. popularity   **5.** equality
6. similarity   **7.** seriousness
8. illness
Understanding Main Ideas: **1.** a
2. b   **3.** c   **4.** c
Remembering Details: **1.** gambling
2. make some big changes   **3.** to be
free   **4.** only their shirts, extremely
cold   **5.** four   **6.** his brother's family
Order of Events: 6, 1, 5, 3, 2, 4
Making Inferences: **1.** a   **2.** c   **3.** b

Unit 5   Sarah Bernhardt
Meaning: **1.** passion   **2.** slap
3. dramatic   **4.** handle   **5.** bizarre
6. debut   **7.** divine   **8.** publicity
9. adore   **10.** prestigious
Extension: **1.** vice versa   **2.** gourmet
3. safari   **4.** chic   **5.** ego   **6.** encore
7. patio   **8.** facade
Understanding Main Ideas: **1.** a
2. a   **3.** b   **4.** a
Remembering Details: **1.** b   **2.** a
3. a   **4.** c   **5.** a   **6.** b
Order of Events: 1, 6, 3, 2, 5, 4
Making Inferences: **1.** b   **2.** a   **3.** c

Unit 6   Nikola Tesla
Meaning: **1.** f   **2.** c   **3.** a   **4.** h
5. b   **6.** j   **7.** e   **8.** d   **9.** i   **10.** g
Extension: **1.** f   **2.** e   **3.** h   **4.** a
5. d   **6.** g   **7.** b   **8.** c
Understanding Main Ideas:
1. a   **2.** c   **3.** b   **4.** b
Remembering Details: **1.** c   **2.** c
3. b   **4.** b   **5.** b   **6.** a

Order of Events: 6, 3, 2, 1, 4, 5
Making Inferences: **1.** a   **2.** c   **3.** c

Unit 7   Sigmund Freud
Meaning: **1.** b   **2.** h   **3.** d   **4.** a
5. i   **6.** g   **7.** f   **8.** j   **9.** e   **10.** c
Extension: happy: delighted, cheerful
sad: depressed, miserable
angry: annoyed, infuriating
scared: terrified, startled
Understanding Main Ideas: **1.** b
2. a   **3.** a   **4.** b
Remembering Details: **1.** b   **2.** b
3. c   **4.** a   **5.** a   **6.** b
Order of Events: 3, 2, 5, 6, 1, 4
Making Inferences: **1.** a   **2.** b   **3.** a

Unit 8   Pandita Ramabai
Meaning: **1.** b   **2.** c   **3.** a   **4.** a
5. b   **6.** c   **7.** c   **8.** b   **9.** a   **10.** b
Extension: **1.** historian   **2.** beautician
3. psychiatrist   **4.** economist
5. Buddhist   **6.** electrician   **7.** chemist
Understanding Main Ideas: **1.** b
2. b   **3.** a   **4.** a
Remembering Details: **1.** She was
treated like a criminal.   **2.** Because
he educated his wife.   **3.** He gave his
money to help the pilgrims.
4. Ramabai could speak seven Indian
dialects and recite 23,000 sacred
verses.   **5.** They read the Sanskrit
writings to large groups of people.
6. Because she had married out of her
class and was a widow with a baby girl.
Order of Events: 4, 1, 2, 3, 5, 6
Making Inferences: **1.** b   **2.** a   **3.** c

Unit 9   Matthew Henson
Meaning: **1.** goal   **2.** expedition
3. credit   **4.** marker   **5.** long for
6. crucial   **7.** assigned   **8.** navigate
9. confirm   **10.** bitter
Extension: **1.** four-door car   **2.** ten-
year-old daughter   **3.** one-week
vacation   **4.** two-hundred page book
5. three-hour meeting   **6.** ten-hour
flight
Understanding Main Ideas: **1.** c
2. a   **3.** a   **4.** b

Remembering Details: **1.** a **2.** c
3. b **4.** b **5.** b
Order of Events: 3, 6, 1, 5, 4, 2
Making Inferences: **1.** b **2.** c **3.** a

Unit 10 Nellie Bly
Meaning: **1.** j **2.** d **3.** f **4.** e
5. a **6.** b **7.** i **8.** c **9.** g **10.** h
Extension: **1.** misspell: to spell
something incorrectly **2.** displease: to
annoy or irritate **3.** mislead: to make
someone believe something that is not
true **4.** misunderstand: to think that
something means one thing when it
means somthing else **5.** discover: to
find something that was hidden or not
known before **6.** discontinue: to stop
7. misjudge: to have the wrong opinion
about something **8.** misinform: to
give someone incorrect information
Understanding Main Ideas: **1.** c
2. a **3.** c **4.** b
Remembering Details: **1.** "What Girls
Are Good For" **2.** Mexico
3. Joseph Pulitzer **4.** mistreatment of
women in prisons, conditions in
factories, divorce, dishonesty in politics
5. returned from her trip around the
world **6.** get away from her troubles
Order of Events: 2, 4, 5, 1, 3, 6
Making Inferences: **1.** b **2.** b **3.** a

Unit 11 Maria Montessori
Meaning: **1.** b **2.** b **3.** a **4.** b
5. c **6.** a **7.** a **8.** c **9.** c **10.** b
Extension: **1.** informal **2.** inability
3. ungrateful **4.** unbelievable **5.** undo
6. unequal **7.** inaccurate
8. unbeatable (Sentences will vary.)
Understanding Main Ideas: **1.** c
2. a **3.** b **4.** c
Remembering Details: **1.** It was one
of the few respectable careers for
young women. **2.** He was very
upset. **3.** Her mother helped her.
4. She gave them activities to do and
things to play with. **5.** She studied
psychology and education.
6. Alexander Graham Bell formed the
American Montessori Society.
Order of Events: 1, 4, 2, 6, 3, 5
Making Inferences: **1.** b **2.** c **3.** c

Unit 12 Jacqueline Cochran
Meaning: **1.** solo **2.** head for
3. master **4.** sack **5.** triumph

6. go on strike **7.** target **8.** fence
9. break a record **10.** status
Extension: **1.** tattoo …tattoos
2. piano …pianos **3.** studio …studios
4. stereo …stereos **5.** hero …heroes
Understanding Main Ideas: **1.** b
2. c **3.** c **4.** b
Remembering Details: **1.** F **2.** T
3. F **4.** T **5.** F **6.** F
Order of Events: 5, 2, 1, 6, 3, 4
Making Inferences: **1.** a **2.** b **3.** c

Unit 13 Althea Gibson
Meaning: **1.** a **2.** c **3.** a **4.** c
5. b **6.** b **7.** a **8.** b **9.** a **10.** c
Extension: **1.** in a row **2.** in charge
of **3.** in case of **4.** in a hurry
5. in private **6.** in fact
Understanding Main Ideas: **1.** b
2. c **3.** c **4.** a
Remembering Details: **1.** They
helped her find a steady job and urged
her to join the local Police Athletic
League sports program. **2.** A musician
named Buddy Walker noticed her talent.
3. Because these clubs did not admit
African Americans. **4.** Alice Marble, a
popular tennis star, helped Althea
Gibson. **5.** She needed to make more
money. **6.** She established the Althea
Gibson Foundation.
Order of Events: 6, 5, 3, 2, 4, 1
Making Inferences: **1.** c **2.** a **3.** a

Unit 14 Gabriel García
Márquez
Meaning: **1.** a **2.** c **3.** a **4.** b
5. b **6.** c **7.** a **8.** c **9.** b **10.** a
Extension: **1.** a **2.** b **3.** b **4.** a
5. a **6.** b
Understanding Main Ideas: **1.** b
2. c **3.** a **4.** a
Remembering Details: **1.** F **2.** T
3. T **4.** F **5.** T **6.** T
Order of Events: 4, 2, 6, 5, 1, 3
Making Inferences: **1.** a **2.** b **3.** a

Unit 15 Dian Fossey
Meaning: **1.** imitate **2.** beat
3. knuckles **4.** mission **5.** unstable
6. aggressive **7.** conduct
8. suspicious **9.** stab **10.** mature
Extension: Head: lash, gums, temple,
jaw, lobe, scalp
Arm and Hand: elbow, wrist, pinkie,
thumb, palm, shoulder

Leg and Foot: sole, heel, shin, ankle,
calf, thigh
Understanding Main Ideas: **1.** b
2. c **3.** c **4.** a
Remembering Details:
1. veterinarian **2.** too old, had no
training **3.** on her knuckles, on wild
plants **4.** was suspicious of her
activities **5.** The Lady Who Lives
Alone in the Forest **6.** fewer and
fewer gorillas
Order of Events: 5, 3, 1, 4, 6, 2
Making Inferences: **1.** a **2.** a **3.** b

Unit 16 Bruce Lee
Meaning: **1.** d **2.** h **3.** b **4.** j
5. f **6.** i **7.** e **8.** a **9.** c **10.** g
Extension: **1.** famous **2.** dangerous
3. ambitious **4.** miraculous
5. nervous **6.** mysterious
Understanding Main Ideas: **1.** c
2. b **3.** a **4.** c
Remembering Details: **1.** c **2.** a
3. b **4.** c **5.** a **6.** a
Order of Events: 5, 1, 2, 3, 4, 6
Making Inferences: **1.** b **2.** a **3.** c

Unit 17 Wilma Mankiller
Meaning: **1.** drought **2.** protest
3. B.A. **4.** inspiration **5.** for good
6. budget **7.** accent **8.** heritage
9. soil **10.** term
Extension: **1.** FBI **2.** UN **3.** RSVP
4. P.S. **5.** PIN **6.** M.A.
Understanding Main Ideas: **1.** c
2. b **3.** c **4.** c
Remembering Details: **1.** F **2.** F
3. F **4.** F **5.** T **6.** T
Order of Events: 2, 1, 6, 4, 3, 5
Making Inferences: **1.** a **2.** b **3.** c

Unit 18 Richard Branson
Meaning: **1.** c **2.** b **3.** a **4.** c
5. b **6.** c **7.** a **8.** a **9.** b **10.** a
Extension: **1.** a fast-moving car
2. a mouth-watering meal **3.** a nice-
looking car **4.** a time-consuming
process **5.** a record-breaking event
6. a far-reaching effect **7.** a good-
looking man **8.** a wood-burning stove
Understanding Main Ideas: **1.** a
2. a **3.** c **4.** b
Remembering Details: **1.** T **2.** T
3. F **4.** F **5.** F
Order of Events: 3, 6, 2, 1, 5, 4
Making Inferences: **1.** c **2.** c **3.** a

Unit 19   Rigoberta Menchú

Meaning: **1.** d   **2.** h   **3.** f   **4.** a
5. i   **6.** c   **7.** g   **8.** j   **9.** b   **10.** e
Extension: **1.** production
2. enjoyment   **3.** employment
4. satisfaction   **5.** government
6. excitement   **7.** improvement
8. pronunciation   **9.** arrangement
10. reaction
Understanding Main Ideas: **1.** c
2. a   **3.** b   **4.** b
Remembering Details: **1.** They took
time off from work to bury the baby.
2. She died because she got sick from
the pesticide spray.   **3.** She left her
job as a servant because she was
treated badly.   **4.** She was hiding in a
church.   **5.** The book was about her
life and the 30-year fight between the
Indians and the military government
of Guatemala.
Order of Events: 2, 4, 6, 3, 5, 1
Making Inferences: **1.** b   **2.** b   **3.** c

Unit 20   Diana Golden

Meaning: **1.** j   **2.** e   **3.** g   **4.** c
5. h   **6.** a   **7.** f   **8.** b   **9.** d   **10.** i
Extension: **1.** go shopping
3. go swimming   **6.** go dancing
8. go running   **10.** go camping
Understanding Main Ideas: **1.** b
2. b   **3.** a   **4.** b
Remembering Details:
1. she could do it by herself
2. leg, back, arms   **3.** a champion and
a hero   **4.** hiking, rock climbing
5. Midnight Sun   **6.** Valentine's Day
Order of Events: 4, 5, 2, 1, 3, 6
Making Inferences: **1.** a   **2.** a   **3.** b

BIBLIOGRAPHY

African American Biography (Vol. 2) (African American Reference Library). Farmington Hills, MI: UXL/Gale Research, Incorporated, 1994.

Altman, Susan. *Extraordinary Black Americans: From Colonial to Contemporary Times.* Danbury: Children's Press/Grolier Publishing, 1989.

Altman, Susan. *The Encyclopedia of African-American Heritage.* New York: Facts on File, 1997.

Ashby, Ruth and Deborah Gore Ohrn, eds. *Herstory: Women Who Changed the World.* New York: Penguin Children's Books, 1995.

Bryant, Mark. *Private Lives: Curious Facts about the Famous and Infamous.* London: Cassell, 1998.

Canning, John, ed. *One Hundred Great Kings and Queens.* New York: Taplinger Publishing, 1968.

Canning, John, ed. *One Hundred Great Modern Lives.* London: Oldham Books, Ltd., 1965.

Chipman, Dawn, Mari Florence, and Naomi Wax. *Cool Women.* Los Angeles: Girl Press, 1998.

Christ, Henry I. *Globe American Biographies.* Upper Saddle River, NJ: Globe Books, 1987.

Deen, Edith. *Great Women of the Christian Faith.* New York: Harper & Brothers Publishers, 1959.

Dewitt, Lisa. *Cue Cards: Famous Women of the Twentieth Century.* Brattleboro, VT: Pro Lingua Associates, 1993.

Facklam, Margaret. *Wild Animals, Gentle Women.* New York and London: Harcourt, Brace, Jovanovich, 1978.

Forbes, Malcolm, and Jeff Bloch. *Women Who Made a Difference.* New York: Simon & Schuster, 1990.

"Gabriel García Márquez." *The Modern Word.* 1999. http://www.the modernword.com/gabo.

Haliwell, Sarah, ed. *The Renaissance.* Austin, TX: Raintree Steck-Vaughn, 1998.

http://www.biography.com. Richard Branson.

Kales, David and Emily Kales. *Masters of Art.* New York: Grosset & Dunlap Publishers, 1967.

Kent, Deborah, and Kathryn Quinlan. *Extraordinary People with Disabilities.* Danbury: Children's Press/Grolier Publishing, 1996.

Krull, Kathleen. *Lives of the Artists: Masterpieces, Messes (And What the Neighbors Thought).* San Diego: Harcourt Trade Publishers, 1995.

Krull, Kathleen. *Lives of the Athletes: Thrills, Spills (And What the Neighbors Thought).* San Diego: Harcourt Trade Publishers, 1997.

Krull, Kathleen. *Lives of the Musicians: Good Times, Bad Times (And What the Neighbors Thought).* San Diego: Harcourt Trade Publishers, 1993.

Landrum, Gene N. *Profiles of Power and Success: Fourteen Geniuses Who Broke the Rules.* Amherst, NY: Prometheus Books, 1996.

Linop, Laurie. *Champions of Equality.* New York: Twenty-first Century Books, 1997.

Littlefield, Bill. *Champions: Stories of Ten Remarkable Athletes.* Boston: Little, Brown and Company, 1993.

Malinowsky, Sharon and Simon Glickman, eds. *Native North American Biography.* Farmington Hills, MI: UXL/Gale Research, Incorporated, 1996.

Marlow, Joan. *The Great Women.* New York: A & W Publishers, Inc. / Hart Associates, 1979.

Mondey, David. *In Profile: Women of the Air.* London: Wayland Publishers, Ltd., 1981.

Price-Groff, Claire. *Extraordinary Women Journalists.* Danbury: Children's Press/Grolier Publishing, 1997.

Rediger, Pat. *Great African Americans in Sports Series.* Calgary: Weigl Educational Publishers, 1996.

Schenittkind, Henry Thomas. *Fifty Great Modern Lives.* New York: Hanover House, 1956.

Schilpp, Madelon Golden. *Great Women of the Press.* Carbondale and Edwardsville, IL: Southern Illinois University Press, 1983.

Schraff, Anne. *Women of Peace.* Springfield, NJ: Enslow Publishers, 1994.

Stille, Darlene. *Extraordinary Women Scientists.* Danbury: Children's Press/Grolier Publishing, 1995.

Thomas, Henry and Dana Lee Thomas. *Living Biographies of Famous Women.* New York: Doubleday, 1952.

Unstead, R.J. *Some Kings and Queens.* Chicago: Follett Publishing, 1962.

Webster's Dictionary of American Women. New York: Smithmark Publishers, 1996.

Welden, Amelie. *Girls Who Rocked the World: Heroines from Sacajawea to Sheryl Swoopes.* Hillsboro, OR: Beyond Words, 1998.